FOLLOW ME

KIM KRISTENSEN

FOLLOW ME
LEADING FROM THE FRONT

maverick
house

Published by Maverick House Publishers in 2017.
First published in Denmark by JP/Politikens Forlagshus in 2015.
This edition is published by agreement with the Kontext Agency.

A CIP catalogue record for this book is available
from the Irish and British Library.

10 9 8 7 6 5 4 3 2 1

Maverick House,
47 Harrington Street,
Dublin 8,
Ireland

www.maverickhouse.com
email: info@maverickhouse.com

ISBN: 978-1-908518-47-7

Contents

Follow Me!

IN NOVEMBER OF 2007 I took one of the most difficult decisions I have ever had to make as a leader.

I was heading up the Danish battalion in Helmand Province in Afghanistan, and as battle group commander I was responsible for the approximately 2,000 Danish, British, Czech and Afghan soldiers who were locked in conflict with the Taliban every single day.

The battle was taking place in perhaps the most dangerous warzone in Afghanistan: the lush, green valley along the Helmand River, popularly called the Green Zone, and which our British predecessors had quite matter-of-factly dubbed 'The Valley of Death'. Unfortunately, the valley lived up to its name. A whole string of fellow soldiers had been killed or wounded since our arrival in August.

It quickly became clear to me that I needed additional resources in the form of main battle tanks. The sixty-three-ton tanks with their night-vision equipment and weaponry would be able to support the infantrymen deployed in the zone, an area of dense vegetation. I saw them as necessary reinforcements that could boost our offensive against the Taliban, saving the lives of many soldiers and Afghans.

Thankfully, there was support back home to meet my request. A platoon with five tanks landed a couple of weeks later in Kandahar, intending to drive as part of a larger convoy through the commercial town of Gereshk and across an important bridge over the Helmand River towards our headquarters in Camp Bastion.

A few days before the convoy was due to embark on the 140-kilometre trip, which for security reasons had to be made in a single stretch – the threat from the Taliban was constant – I was approached by a few worried-looking staff officers.

'We've got a problem,' they said.

'What kind of problem?' I asked.

'A big one,' came the reply. 'We can't guarantee that the bridge will hold!'

I took a deep breath and had to swallow more than once while they explained that the bridge, which had been built during the Soviet occupation and was one of southern Afghanistan's main transport routes, was classified as suitable for vehicles no heavier than 45 tons. In other words, although the tanks would be crossing the bridge one by one, we would still be well over the maximum weight limit.

'We can't let that happen,' I thought. Of all the news I had been given day after day by my staff of thirty-seven experts, this information was perhaps the most unpleasant. The pressure on our soldiers in the Green Zone was enormous. Sending in tanks to support them as soon as possible was, as I say, a matter of life and death. And now I was being told they couldn't cross a bridge without the risk of collapse. That just couldn't be right!

My first impulse was to ask my staff, and the engineering specialists they had consulted, to take another look at the situation. Was it possible they had overlooked something? Maybe their analysis was wrong?

It was wishful thinking, perhaps largely motivated by the desire – common among leaders in high-pressure situations – to buy myself some time. They were well aware of the enormous responsibility on their shoulders, so naturally they had already been thorough, and the message remained the same: 'We can't guarantee that the bridge will hold, commander.'

In war there are rules dictating what a leader can and can't do. But if needs must, he or she can choose to waive them. In practice, this means that I could have decided to make an emergency reclassification of the bridge in light of the operative urgency, ordering the tanks to drive over it as originally planned.

The problem was that we weren't talking about a few extra tons. We were right up against the edge of what was possible.

That was the situation. There was no more advice to be had from my staff. There was no way round it. I *had* to make a decision.

Finding an alternative route, if that were even possible, would have been time-consuming, logistically challenging and very risky. It would increase the likelihood of an attack by the Taliban. If I decided that the tanks should 'wade' (or swim) across the powerful Helmand River, they might be swept away by the current. Moreover, the soldiers in the warzone were in desperate and immediate need of them.

On the other hand, if the bridge collapsed the consequences would be catastrophic. First and foremost, of course, it would be disastrous for the team in the individual tank, who would most likely be killed, and devastating for their relatives.

It would also be a major national scandal. There had been some opposition in certain military and political circles to deploying tanks. Just imagine the fallout if they went crashing through one of the country's most important bridges before they had even made it to their destination. It would put my decision in a very bad light. They might justifiably ask whether we had reconnoitred the area at all, and it would cast a dark shadow over the Danish military presence in Afghanistan – maybe even over the Danish armed forces as a whole.

Moreover, a collapsed bridge would be a catastrophe for the area. If we cut off a major transport route and paralysed the infrastructure in southern Afghanistan, it would be difficult for people to transport their goods. It would cause an uproar and could easily trigger unrest.

And for me, personally? When you're in a leadership position during a time of war, you have to take decisions every day that could mean the loss of human life. This was a decision that – if it went wrong – would forever overshadow everything else in my career, no matter what I had done before and no matter what I did next.

My mind raced. I thought about the soldiers in the tanks. I thought about the soldiers in the valley. I thought about their loved-ones. I thought about the potential political consequences – national and international. I weighed up the pros and cons – and then I made my decision:

'We're driving over the bridge!'

All possible precautions were taken. The whole thing was planned down to the tiniest detail, as military operations always are. The bridge would be crossed at the dead of night, to minimise the threat from the Taliban. The tanks would cross one at a time, driving at a consistent, low speed. They mustn't turn and they mustn't come to a sudden halt.

The operation was a success! The bridge held! On 12 November 2007, a little before six o'clock, the convoy – with the five tanks at its head – arrived at our headquarters in Camp Bastion. It was a relief, of course. But I was even more pleased when the tanks proved their value just a week later, when they were first deployed. They made exactly the impact – for the remainder of that year and the next – that our analysis had predicted they would.

Why did I choose to start the book with this story?

Because it highlights the fact that, as leaders, we have final responsibility. I have met many dynamic and talented leaders in the worlds of business and industry, sport and culture, and in local authorities whose mindset is clearly orientated towards consensus. When a decision has to be made, they always prefer to reach an agreement. They are used to decisions being taken after extensive group discussion; everybody has to be involved, and there must be agreement about the issue in question.

This is all perfectly fine. I have great respect for involvement and group work, often using these methods myself, but I firmly believe that when it comes to making serious decisions, enough is enough. There can only be one person in charge. What I feel is lacking with many leaders is the courage to stand on the front line

> I have great respect for involvement and group work, often using these methods myself, but I firmly believe that when it comes to making serious decisions, enough is enough. There can only be one person in charge.

and say, 'Follow me'. Quite the contrary – instead their attitude is more like, 'Off you go, I'm right behind you'. In the long run, this approach is not sustainable.

In Afghanistan I had a talented and loyal staff who told me what I needed to know, including the less palatable information. But they didn't want to push me in a particular direction. They expected me to make decisions based on the information they provided.

The worst thing I could have done would have been to try and drag an opinion out of them: 'Don't you reckon it's a good idea to reclassify the bridge and let the tanks drive over it? How nice that we're all in agreement about this ...'.

It doesn't work. Let me emphasise this again: when the going gets tough, there's only one person in charge.

I'm well aware that there's a difference between being a commander in a war and a manager at a company, an organisation or a public authority. Very few managerial decisions are literally a matter of life and death. But I still believe that experiences of leadership under extreme circumstances – and a war is certainly that – can be used to the benefit of all leaders and managers.

It has been my experience that many managers find it difficult to lead from the front and make themselves visible, especially when things get tough. But it's in precisely those situations that it's important to step forward and choose a direction, to be able to be honest even when delivering terrible news, and to take the repercussions.

As a leader, always being there when times get tough for your employees is a long-term investment.

As a leader, always being there when times get tough for your employees is a long-term investment: if you're with them when the danger is at its worst, then they will be there for you when you need them.

It's easy to say 'follow me' when things are going well – what inspires confidence and trust is being able to say it even when they're not. This is what really tests a leader's mettle.

It's easy to say 'follow me' when things are going well – what inspires confidence and trust is being able to say it even when they're not.

I have long wanted to share my experiences of leadership – primarily in the armed forces, but also from the worlds of business, diplomacy, the Danish royal court and elsewhere – because I have found that they can be inspirational for other leaders. I also see it as my duty to pass on my experience. Few leaders have been as privileged as I have. I have gained experience in many different fields, and since 1997 I have been jotting down notes about them. As a result, a clear picture has emerged over the years of what it takes to excel as a leader, whether you are an officer, an executive, a theatre manager or an ambassador. Not just to succeed, but to truly excel.

My six years' tenure at the Danish royal court – initially as adjutant to Her Majesty the Queen and most recently as the Master of Ceremonies – has given me additional inspiration around the subject of leadership, as well as organisational and strategic development. When you're on a state visit led by the royal family and accompanied by various ministers and delegates from the worlds of business and culture, you're very much part of 'branding' Denmark. It has been instructive and incredibly rewarding to experience how a nation can gather its strength for a state visit to, for instance, China.

I am now ready to put down my experiences in writing.

In this book I emphasise eight points that I have found to be crucial – absolutely crucial – in order to excel as a leader. I have focused on the kind of leadership necessary to be among the very best, drawing on what I have witnessed in the military, local government, and the worlds of business and diplomacy.

These eight points are thrown into the sharpest relief when lives are at stake – when you are at war – and this is why I still maintain that the greatest source of leadership inspiration for me is what I learned and experienced as an officer during wartime. This conviction is reflected in the narrative of the book. But because I have used these eight points in briefing, teaching and sharing information outside the armed forces, I know that they can be inspirational for many others.

During the war I met many younger officers and sergeants who, even under the worst conceivable conditions, were capable of taking a heavy rucksack from an exhausted soldier, slinging it over their shoulder and saying, 'Follow me!'

I have the utmost respect for these officers and sergeants, who were caring enough to take ultimate responsibility for younger soldiers, showing great professional competence, physical strength and profound courage. Those are the kinds of officers and sergeants that soldiers are willing to follow through fire and water, day in, day out, week after week, despite the risk to their lives. They were my greatest inspiration as I wrote this book. It is among them that I saw genuine leaders: people who chose to lead their soldiers by going first.

It is my hope that you will be inspired, challenged and motivated by reading this book about leadership under extreme circumstances – that you will 'translate' it into your own activities as a leader, laying the groundwork so that one day your employees will be prepared to follow you, too, through fire and water.

It is also my hope that you are willing to be open and to commit yourself, applying these ideas to yourself and your own activities as a leader. The book focuses on personal leadership, based on a strong professional background. You will be challenged to consider a leadership style in which you must be willing to go first, take the heaviest rucksack and dare to say 'follow me', all while showing the utmost care and consideration for your employees.

If you choose this style of leadership, there's no getting around it: you have to be brave!

CHAPTER 1

Lead From the Front

'**I NEED** two volunteers to walk through a minefield with me! Who's up for it?'

Asking this question of the soldiers in the reconnaissance section I was with in the former Yugoslavia probably sounds crazy, so let me rewind a little and explain why it was necessary.

In February of 1995 I took responsibility for 166 soldiers – Danes and Lithuanians – sent on a peace-keeping operation to Croatia, specifically Krajina, near the border with Bosnia and Herzegovina. As the term suggests, our task was to keep the peace.

But peace was fragile. It only lasted three weeks! Shortly after our arrival, both the Croatian and Serbian troops returned to their old battle positions, in many places only a few hundred metres from each other. Every day there were confrontations and shots exchanged, and both parties began to place mines in the no-man's-land between them.

It all came to a head on 4 August at around five in the morning, when the Croatian forces attacked the Serbs in Krajina. Two-hundred thousand Serbs were forced to flee the area. In September the Croatians conducted another military offensive. Three Danish soldiers were killed in battle, and several others were wounded.

The problem was that our mandate wasn't appropriate for the situation in which we now found ourselves. There was no longer any question of peace-keeping. We were in a warzone, which meant that for months we had to live with the risk of being caught in the crossfire between the Serbs and the Croatians.

Neither side really wanted us to abandon our positions, so my soldiers ended up as hostages in a situation that – perhaps – nobody could have foreseen. Many of our outposts were literally in no-man's-land, directly in the firing-line between the Croatians and the Serbs, who had laid mines around several of them.

One outpost was particularly exposed. It was isolated, and the dirt road that led to it was no longer usable because the whole area was mined. The soldiers situated there were running low on food and water. It was uncomfortably hot, and they were in danger of dehydrating. When access to food and water is inadequate, your chances of falling ill increase. Over the radio, we knew from the sergeant in charge at the outpost that they were under pressure. The situation wasn't critical, but it would quickly become so if we didn't do something. We inquired about the possibility of bringing in helicopter assistance, but sending them into the area was judged to be too much of a risk.

So I gathered the reconnaissance section together. This unit contained some of our most skilled soldiers, and they knew the area like the back of their hand.

'We've got to get to our comrades. They're in need of water, food and medicine. That means we're going through a minefield. I don't know how big it is, or what kind of mines are in it. I'm going myself, but I need two volunteers to come with me.'

Every single hand was raised. All of them, without exception. So in consultation with the section commander I chose the two soldiers we judged to be best suited to the task.

How is it possible that, as someone in command of 166 soldiers, I took the – objectively speaking, foolish – decision to sling a rucksack with fresh rations on my back and walk into a minefield, risking being blown up and leaving a unit without a commander, when I could have ordered somebody else to do it without a raised eyebrow?

It's a good question, and I've given it a good deal of thought. The best answer I can give is: I couldn't help it.

It wasn't a decision I took after a lengthy process of analysis. I barely gave it a second thought; it was just obvious that that was how it had to be. I felt an obligation to the soldiers and their relatives. I couldn't let them down!

I also felt that, quite simply, my presence might convey the seriousness of the situation to the Croatian and Serbian commandants. I hoped they would understand that our access to the outposts had to be made easier and more secure. Sadly, that turned out to be wishful thinking.

On our way to the isolated soldiers we stopped at a Serbian control post, after which we had to walk three or four kilometres before reaching the headquarters of the Croatian commandant. I had a personal connection with him, so I knew I could turn up the pressure.

'I want you to guide us through your minefield so that we can reach my soldiers. They urgently need food, water and medicine. If things go wrong, and I or my two soldiers are killed on the way, the whole world will find out that your side is responsible.'

He looked surprised, but agreed to my request. He himself accompanied us and got his people to lead us through.

However, when we were about 300 yards away from the outpost, he stopped and said:

'We've laid mines up to this point. I can guarantee there are no more of ours. But I don't know what the Serbs have done in the next stretch.'

Clearly this wasn't good news. The result was that the two scouts with me had to stick their bayonets in the ground to detect any further mines between us and the outpost, and if they hit a mine they would have to carefully brush the earth away. This kind of work is so physically and psychologically strenuous that it's virtually impossible to imagine the kind of pressure we were under. I followed hard on their heels, carrying the rucksack with the water, food and medicine.

When, at one point, I found myself standing with my legs placed either side of a mine, it occurred to me that we had stumbled into a ridiculous situation – this was supposed to be a peace-keeping mission.

Some of what crossed my mind was more personal, too. I thought about my family; in the left top pocket of my uniform I was carrying pictures of my wife Tine and our first son Frederik. He was only one-and-a-half years old, and I had just received a new photo of him. One week earlier, Tine had told me she was pregnant, so I knew that baby number two was on the way. As we moved slowly towards the outpost, my family was constantly on my mind, but other, stranger thoughts kept popping up too: would somebody find the two photos in my top pocket if we got blown up by a mine? During the mission to Afghanistan in 2007, we all wrote goodbye letters and passed on our final instructions and wishes if the worst should happen. We didn't do that back in 1995, so it was important to me that the photos would, at least, be found.

At the same time, I was acutely aware that we couldn't turn back. The soldiers at the outpost could follow our progress with the naked eye as we laboriously cleared a path. The rest of the company was listening over the radio. If we turned back, all my credibility and all the confidence they had in me as a leader would be shattered in a heartbeat.

It took a few hours to cover the final 300 yards, but we managed it safely. The relief and happiness was indescribable. The soldiers in the isolated outpost have never forgotten the situation:

'When things got tricky, when we were really in trouble, the commander himself came to us with a rucksack on his back.'

It reinvigorated morale among the whole company. They knew that they'd have someone in their corner should they find themselves in difficulty. We had cleared a path to the outpost, which remained clear. And we had sent a strong signal to the Croatians that they had to respect our presence and be considerate of our safety.

> If we turned back, all my credibility and all the confidence they had in me as a leader would be shattered in a heartbeat.

I was thirty years old when I was given responsibility for the mission with the Danish and Lithuanian soldiers, and it taught me an incredible amount about leadership. One point stands out from the others, however, and it has proved critical for success many times since then: you have to lead from the front. You have to go first. In good times, but especially in bad.

I have seen many officers and sergeants take on far more difficult and dangerous missions than my walk through the minefield in Krajina. Since the mid-1990s, when Danish troops first became involved in dangerous and challenging long-term operations in some of the world's most dangerous conflict zones, I have witnessed as a natural development this generation of leaders grow accustomed to taking ultimate responsibility – to going first. There is a principle of leadership that overshadows all other principles: that of leading by example. The power of doing so is loud and clear; it's obvious to all if you're leading from the front or sitting safe and sound in your office.

The leadership courses I have conducted for private businesses, local authorities and so on have always had this point on the agenda. The courses focused on coaching and developing leaders to take responsibility, step up and get involved. This is how you separate the good leaders from the bad.

There is a principle of leadership that overshadows all other principles: that of leading by example.

You build trust and credibility among your employees if they know that you'll be there – not just at the office party but when serious illness strikes, the stock price tanks, orders are lost and people's jobs are cut.

Sadly, I have also seen leaders reveal themselves not to be such at all, just as the tough decisions need to be communicated to their employees. My message to the people I have been responsible for training, coaching and developing is simple and straightforward: you need to step up!

Your employees may not be especially happy with you at that moment, but over time you will build respect for yourself and your leadership. This is the long-term investment I mentioned in the foreword.

Many managers, as discussed above, find it hard to assume this role. Who doesn't recognise the type of leader who sends lieutenants into the field instead of delivering bad news themselves? I've certainly known a few, and I can only say that, over time, they lose out when judged against the most important measure of them all: the day they need to say 'follow me' to their employees, they will glance back over their shoulder and see that, yes, they're certainly going first. However, they're also going it alone. Their employees have hung back.

But how do you know when the time has come to step up, be visible and 'go first'?

In my experience it's often about intuition and trusting your gut. It'll come to you. If you're thinking that you probably don't have this kind of intuition, then become better acquainted with your employees: show interest and spend time with them, listen to their representatives and committees. If you're an honest leader and not a fake one, you'll receive help from those around you. If your staff have confidence in you – and you are listening – they will become a vital sounding board.

If you're a fan of 'Rambo'-style leadership, where you're perpetually trying to seem strong, invulnerable and cool, then I'm sorry to disappoint you – when a crisis first arises you should be prepared for many people not to follow you. You won't be able to excel in a crisis. I've seen it often, with both younger and older managers: if you're 'playing' the role of leader rather than actually being one, the whole effect will be artificial and untrustworthy.

For a while I was involved with a large Danish corporation, where I had the opportunity to shadow senior staff (the management and board of directors). There were several moments when tough decisions needed to be taken – almost every day, in fact – including one regarding a massive set of job cuts at an overseas plant. There was no question that the managing director, the CEO, should deliver the news in person at the plant, but he was persuaded by the other managers and directors that it was more important to remain in Denmark to field questions from the press. He sent his 'lieutenants' to the city to deliver the bad news.

It was clear to me that he wanted to avoid confrontation. But he shouldn't have. He should have stepped up, because the consequences within the company were obvious. He let them down, and all confidence in him as a leader was destroyed.

Whenever I have spent time at the front with our soldiers – as a commander in Afghanistan, for example – one thing that I have found to be true, and which has remained impossible for me to ignore, is that if I'm always going to be ready to step up when a crisis hits, then it's incredibly important for me to feel that there is something to stand up for. But it's also incredibly important that there is someone to stand up for. That I know I can rely on my commanders and that I respect both their professionalism and them as people. If that's not the case, you won't get me to lead soldiers through a hail of bullets to achieve a particular goal.

In Afghanistan I had British commanders in whom I had that kind of confidence. At home in Denmark I had the head of the Danish army, Major General Poul Kiærskou. As mentioned, I had to take many difficult and critical decisions, but never during a mission did I feel that he would wash his hands of the situation if something went wrong. Never!

Having a boss like that was crucial if I wanted to perform well as a leader, so I felt extremely privileged.

The overriding goal was to eliminate the Taliban so that the Afghan people could have a chance to live their lives. This was a goal I felt strongly about. So I had both some*thing* and some*one* to stand up for.

As a commander placed under extraordinary pressure, I experienced other aspects of my superiors back home in Denmark. Leaders who always had to hedge

If I'm always going to be ready to step up when a crisis hits, then it's incredibly important for me to feel that there is something and someone to stand up for.

their bets and those who revealed through their choice of words that they'd be queuing up to wash their hands if things went south: 'There does seem to be a risk of ...' meant: 'I pointed this out, I warned you ...'. That's the kind of boss you try to put behind you – but you don't forget them, because you know you won't go into battle for them if you can help it.

However, it wasn't at headquarters that the best examples of 'follow me'-style leadership unfolded in practice, but out in the deserts of Helmand, among the young officers and sergeants. They didn't come from special operations units. They were apparently quite ordinary young Danish men and women from regiments like the Royal Life Guards, the Guard Hussar Regiment, the Dragoon Regiment and other units in the Danish armed forces, but I can tell you that they were anything but ordinary. These young officers and sergeants proved to be role models for their soldiers in the heat of battle, when faced with enormous challenges.

Let me tell you about a concrete episode involving one such young officer, an episode that also illustrates how important it is to maintain a laser-like focus on the task you've been assigned.

It took place on one of our final days in Afghanistan, and the leader in question was a young platoon commander, an exceptionally talented and highly respected officer who was responsible for thirty soldiers. After six months at the front in Helmand, the soldiers were physically and mentally drained – virtually crushed by exhaustion. The weather had been a constant challenge, ranging from fifty degrees in the summer to minus twenty in January. They had been in countless tough clashes and lived under constant threat from the Taliban. By this point, most of them had lost around ten kilos. They had conducted themselves in exemplary fashion, and were due their share of the credit for ensuring that the Taliban no longer had control over the Upper Gereshk Valley. Now, frankly, all they were looking forward to was going home.

I considered it necessary for the platoon to complete one final, difficult task: a foot patrol in an area previously overrun by the Taliban. The aim was to ensure that they had not come back, so we were going to check on the Afghan families who had returned, and assess the situation.

The platoon commander answered that his unit was worn out after six months at war, which was true. They didn't have much strength left. My response was necessary and quite clear: I understood what he was saying, but the assignment was important and had to be done, which he accepted without further ado.

From a distance, I could see him gathering his platoon and telling them about the new assignment. I could see the tiredness in the soldiers' faces, and sense their frustration at being given yet another difficult and dangerous task. The platoon commander concluded his short briefing by saying that he was about to start getting his equipment ready, and that he would soon be heading out on the assignment – alone, if necessary. With incredible concentration and focus, he began to prepare his equipment and, slowly but surely, the rest of the unit followed suit. He was the first person ready to leave the camp, and he simply stood and waited. When he could see that everyone was nearly ready, he began – calmly but with great physical presence – to walk towards the exit. It was a quiet demonstration that gave the soldiers who weren't quite ready the last push they needed to get a move on. I never doubted for a moment they would follow him. The way he physically demonstrated his willingness to carry out the assignment was a perfect example of the 'follow me' style of leadership. The unit was utterly worn out, as was the platoon commander himself. It was moments like that – and there were many of them – where I witnessed first-hand absolutely first-class leadership. The soldiers followed their platoon commander because they didn't want to let him down, just as he hadn't let them down during many fierce bouts of fighting.

As senior leaders, we must be uncomfortably aware that the battle is won by 'platoon commanders'. We can lay out a framework and make plans, but it's carrying them out that produces results. That's the business end of leadership, delivering results in the military, in industry, in local government and in schools.

Do we always focus enough on that?

There was a photo taken of the platoon after they had returned from the assignment in one piece. It's a fantastic picture depicting tiredness, relief, happiness and pride.

As senior leaders, we must be uncomfortably aware that the battle is won by 'platoon commanders'.

Several times I've heard the power of example – or terms like role model – mentioned as something to watch out for. A good few years ago there was much discussion of the dangers inherent in putting someone on a pedestal and saying, 'that's what you should be like, that's the right thing to do, you should be more like him or her.' I never understood that debate. I think it's utter nonsense. The bottom line is that, whether as a soldier or a company employee, when you encounter an example of good leadership – competent, caring and involved – it can dramatically raise your game.

We have all met somebody we look up to, respect deeply and want to be like. I can't see anything wrong with that. I have deliberately spent a lot of time on my courses talking about role models. In 2014 I gave a management-training course at a large Finnish company. At one point I asked the participants to write down the name of the person they looked up to the most. It could be anybody from a boss to their mother or an old football coach. Afterwards, they were supposed to come up with five reasons why they chose that person.

The most common reasons can be summed up in a single word: *decency*!

They placed a lot of emphasis on the individual being a good listener, interested in others, and fundamentally a caring, affectionate, supportive and ethical person. Qualities like professional competence, financial wizardry or excellent communication skills were also mentioned.

I meet a lot of people who think that military leadership is all about rigid discipline. Nothing could be further from the truth. If you insist on nothing but strict discipline during wartime, you die. I'll expand on this in a later chapter, but at the moment I want to emphasise that good leadership is about providing a framework and resources, presenting an intention and a goal to be realised, and then giving leaders the opportunity to accomplish their task. We can't be peering over each other's shoulders twenty-four hours a day, so trusting your leaders is what gets results. As those in charge higher up the ladder, we select and train the leaders who end up on the front lines (whether within the police, the school system, local and national government, businesses or anywhere else) to live up to these expectations. If they can't, then they must be given further training; it's not enough to rely on guidelines, however good they are, or on a system of checks and balances to ensure good leadership. Administration and management, perhaps but not leadership. Leadership has to do with people, and the relationship created between leaders and employees is crucial for success.

This is why rigid discipline doesn't work. If all leaders got used to being micro-managed, the creative, innovative and action-orientated ones would disappear. And if those qualities disappear from leaders on the front lines, you'll never win a war.

I meet a lot of people who think that military leadership is all about rigid discipline. Nothing could be further from the truth.

Ultimately, this means that good leadership is about being a decent person, about going first and setting a good example. Your employees have to feel like you're on their side. Otherwise, you can throw as many resources as you like at bonus schemes, fruit baskets, longer holidays or any other tactic in the HR toolkit without any guarantee that your employees will follow you when it comes to the crunch.

From my perspective, the financial crisis has been a blessing for businesses. Those who have kept an eye out for successful leaders during this tough time – the business equivalent of wartime – will be able to develop their management team with this knowledge in mind: they will have seen who their employees turn to in a crisis, who they rely on and trust.

Similarly fundamental is whether a leader has a healthy degree of self-belief, and can say, like Major Anders Storrud, who was a company commander during my tenure as battle group commander in Helmand, and who with his 150 soldiers was deployed on the front lines against the Taliban:

'You should never make your soldiers do anything you wouldn't do yourself!'

Anders Storrud was one of the best officers I have ever met. Professionally speaking he was highly competent, but he also had a special capacity to show compassion for his soldiers. He proved himself both in Kosovo and Iraq. He delivered when there was a need for clear directives and orders, but was also there when it came time to put a comforting arm around a soldier who was struggling. It would be an understatement to say that Anders was respected. He was loved by his soldiers.

When I had to find someone to put in charge of the company, which was about to be deployed on the front line of the military operation against the Taliban, I had no doubt whatsoever that Anders Storrud was the best man for the job. On 26 September 2007, some soldiers in that company found themselves hard pressed: one section, situated at an exposed outpost in the flat marshland by the Helmand River, came under attack around 9pm.

I was at the company headquarters in a nearby patrol base, and witnessed Anders' deliberations and decision-making first-hand. I was impressed by the calmness of his demeanour as he issued orders to his troops. From the company headquarters we could hear and feel the intensity of the conflict. The outpost was under heavy attack.

The situation took a dramatic turn when we discovered that several soldiers had been wounded. Our intelligence sources informed us that the Taliban was going to try and surround the outpost, attacking it with the intention of taking our soldiers hostage. Shortly afterwards we became especially nervous when the section commander at the outpost itself suddenly stopped responding to radio communications. We feared the worst, but luckily it turned out that he had narrowly avoided being hit, and had to take a moment to sort out the unit and himself. Our relief was short-lived, however. The message came over the radio: two of our soldiers had been killed.

'You should never make your soldiers do anything you wouldn't do yourself!'

It was a crushing blow, compounded by the fact that the fighting at the outpost was becoming more and more intense. There was a very real risk of further losses – indeed it was entirely possible that the whole section of twelve men might be killed or captured.

Deep in concentration, Anders Storrud weighed all this up, considering how best to support them from the command post and issuing his directives with no hesitation in his voice, but when the situation finally came to a head he left his post and advanced towards me, his steps purposeful and his gaze steady. I already knew what he was going to say:

'Commander, I'm going out there!'

It didn't sound like a question or an invitation for discussion, but rather a precise statement, which he spoke with great determination.

In that situation I experienced one of war's many dilemmas. On the one hand, there were plenty of good arguments for him staying at the command post and organising operations from there, rather than setting out on a dangerous journey and risking being hit. If something went wrong, it would be easy to point the finger afterwards. On the other hand, I knew that when soldiers' lives are threatened, they need their commander to be present. He can help calm things down simply by being there. A clap on the shoulder or an acknowledging nod can make a world of difference under pressure. I was in no doubt that I should trust his instincts and back him up. Anders wouldn't let down his soldiers, so my answer was brief:

'Yes, Anders, you are!'

The soldiers were literally queuing up to accompany him, and at great risk to their own lives they set out in the dark on an hour-long journey through fields of metre-high maize before finally reaching the outpost, where the situation had now started to stabilise.

Could Anders and a handful of soldiers have fought down the Taliban? No, they probably couldn't. But the mere fact of his presence gave them a morale boost. Afterwards the soldiers said it was like having a colossal burden lifted when they suddenly saw the company commander standing in their midst. He knew he wasn't the kind of boss who let other people do the dirty work. He was ready 'to take his share of the crap', as one of them later remarked.

And at least as important is that he knew he would still be there when his soldiers were hit – now, tomorrow, the next day and always.

By around three in the morning Anders Storrud and the other soldiers were back at headquarters with the unit that had lost two of its comrades. Most of them collapsed in exhaustion and fell asleep. We were all grief-stricken. I took a walk around the company camp to see whether anybody needed support. It was then that I noticed a light coming from an armoured personnel carrier. When I got closer, I could see that Anders was in there all alone. He was writing some commemorative words about the fallen soldiers, and personal letters to their loved-ones – letters that would accompany the coffins home.

This was another one of those situations where, as the person in charge, you have to take the lead. You can't palm off that job onto somebody else. But it isn't easy. What can you write that would be meaningful and lessen the pain – even just a little – of those left behind? No wonder he was surrounded by dozens of balled-up drafts of the letters.

That night we talked about what it meant to be a leader. To not let people down. To be wherever was most difficult. To go first. My respect for Anders was so great that I was able to say quite calmly that he was the best leader his soldiers could have wished for in that tough situation.

When it comes to leadership, the world of the military is extreme and final. It's not, like some people think, a question of sitting safe and sound in an auditorium, talking about leadership with regular breaks. Discussion and theoretical understanding are necessary and rewarding, but it's through harsh experience and in war itself that real leaders emerge.

Leadership in a time of war is bloody, dirty and frightening, often executed under fire. You must never forget this when selecting and training leaders who will be active in a warzone, because you would be letting down the leaders who are already deployed there. But does this apply only to officers and sergeants in wartime?

In my experience, the fundamental principles of leadership necessary in order to excel are precisely the same in the worlds of art, sports, business, local government and the royal court.

No, it does not. In my experience, the fundamental principles of leadership necessary in order to excel are precisely the same in the worlds of art, sports, business, local government and the royal court: the ability to go first, especially when doing so is unpleasant. The ability to be caring towards your employees. The ability to give them something and someone to stand up for. Exactly the same leadership tools, frameworks and terms apply whenever it is necessary to excel.

In the next chapter I will focus on the framework that needs to be in place so that you have something to stand up for. It's about developing a unique strategy. Think about the following sentence before you plunge into the next chapter. I will return to it, because it is deeply important when it comes to the hard, laborious work of forming a strategy.

'You have to be able to live with yourself for the rest of your life!'

CHAPTER 2

Create a Unique Strategy

IN THE EARLY summer of 2007 myself and a small group of senior officers were busy planning and preparing a strategy for our deployment in Helmand, where as battle group commander I would be responsible for military operations in the central part of the province.

We knew we were heading into a tough conflict. The Taliban were deeply embedded in the river valley north of the commercial town of Gereshk, and it was our job to put them on the defensive, creating the conditions necessary for civilian life – trade, schools, medical clinics and infrastructure – to reassert itself in Gereshk and the surrounding area.

Thankfully, I was given an ideal framework to start from. I could hand-pick the most talented people for each position and was allocated the necessary resources for training and development. But was it enough to accomplish our task? Did we have the right professional skills in place? Were we physically fit enough? Were we approaching the job ahead of us with the mindset you need for war – to keep up the momentum and know that you can never take your foot off the gas?

While working on the strategy we focused closely on the details, analysing every situation, whether conceivable or inconceivable. In the military world, being responsible for a strategy also means being responsible for the lives of those carrying it out. This knowledge is constantly on your mind as you deliberate, trying to come up with the best possible plan. You think about your soldiers and their loved-ones, you think about the local population you're there to help, and you think about the opponents you're

In the military world, being responsible for a strategy also means being responsible for the lives of those carrying it out. This knowledge is constantly on your mind as you deliberate, trying to come up with the best possible plan.

fighting. You think, too, that you can't come second place in wartime. If you're in second place, you're dead. It sounds a bit flippant to put it like that, but unfortunately that's the reality, and it's perfectly serious. You bear that knowledge in mind as you work on your strategy.

From the first, it was crystal clear to me that we mustn't make the same mistake as when I was deployed as company commander in the Balkans in 1995. In Krajina we weren't prepared for war. We couldn't influence events ourselves, so instead we just had to wait and see what the Serbs and Croatians would come up with. We were reactive, without the authority or organisational structure to intervene; indeed, we could hardly look after ourselves. This passivity meant that officers dropped the ball. They neglected their responsibility to protect the vulnerable, the weak and the persecuted. You have a duty to intervene when it comes to blatant injustice, no matter whose authority you're operating under. I never forgot what it felt like to be let down like that, so I made a decision: if I ever found myself in a war again, I would be sure to take the initiative. If you are too reactive, it's only a matter of time before that rebounds on you. As far as possible, it's always better to adopt an offensive and active strategy.

Does deciding to take an active and offensive approach mean that you're obsessed with war? Not at all. It's purely a matter of analysis. When speed is a key parameter in terms of who strikes first and hardest, that must necessarily be reflected in the strategy you adopt.

In Helmand we wanted to be a step ahead of the Taliban at all times, both mentally and practically. We had to be focused about how we used the resources at our disposal, both temporally and geographically. There is a Norwegian phrase – *hensynsløs kraftsamling* – which roughly translates as 'ruthless, concentrated force'. The Americans use the term focused violence. Or, to put it another way: it's more effective to hit someone with your fist than with an open hand.

This may sound harsh, but it's rooted in the desire to strike hard and fast, and – not least – with precision. Above all, we want to strike the people we're targeting and avoid hurting innocent civilians. It's crucial to bear this in mind when you're aiming for *hensynsløs kraftsamling* or *focused violence*.

I've seen the same approach used in many other areas outside the military world, although obviously the precise terms vary. If, for instance, a private company wants to launch a new product or enter a new market, this too requires laser-like focus and the concentrated application of means and resources.

On 11 May 2007, a few months before we were due to arrive in Helmand and while the strategic planning was still in full flow, my staff officers requested a meeting at the Royal Life Guards' barracks in Høvelte, in the Danish region of North Zealand. They wanted to keep me apprised about a number of issues that had cropped up.

I noticed that the chaplain was present during the briefing. This was unusual, but I thought no more about it as they presented me with an array of operative, logistical and security-related problems to contend with. The last point on the chief of staff's list was the following:

'In light of the military operations we are to carry out in Helmand, the physical and weather-related challenges we will face, and the strength of the Taliban, I must conclude that our unit has too few coffins. We should have more coffins ready.'

I have been given many briefings over the years, but this was one I will never forget. Outwardly I kept my composure, but I could feel a physical reaction in my body at the chief of staff's words. I had been in no doubt as to the seriousness of our mission before the briefing, but the analytical and strategic preparations the chief of staff had run through in detail lent it extra weight. 'We're not bringing enough coffins!' It wasn't the kind of problem I had learned to deal with as a young cadet at the military academy. Imagine what would happen if we lost ten soldiers at a single stroke and we didn't have enough coffins!

This kind of unflinching strategic planning also ended up influencing the briefings I gave soldiers' relatives across Denmark over the summer. As I stood in front of 150 people one day in June, in a packed auditorium at the Varde Barracks in Jutland, I was determined to avoid another mistake I had made twelve years earlier, just before our deployment to Krajina.

I had promised all those families that their loved-ones would come home. Deep down both they and I knew, of course, that I couldn't promise that. That it was mainly wishful thinking on my part. Three Danish soldiers lost their lives during Operation Oluja ('Storm') and Operation Una, which was a Croatian-led military offensive against the Krajina Serbs that took place in August and September 1995. Other Danish soldiers were wounded, and still others sustained psychological damage with which many are struggling even today. Everybody in my company did, in fact, make it home, but far from all of them emerged psychologically unscathed. I was forced to acknowledge that my promise had been empty: I couldn't tell them with certainty that we would all make it home in good shape. So I took a decision: if I ever went to war again, I would be brutally honest with both the soldiers and their relatives. My message that summer's day in Varde was therefore as follows:

'I must make it clear to you that we are undertaking an incredibly hard and dangerous mission. For the first time since 1864, the Danish army is being deployed in long-term offensive operations. For this reason I must also tell you that I don't think all of us will come home.'

A faint murmur ran through the auditorium. I could feel a particular intensity in the air. There was no doubt that the seriousness of the situation was sinking in. There were also scattered outbursts of emotion. The wives, girlfriends and children clearly needed to be comforted afterwards. I myself had a long conversation with a teenage girl, who told me with tears in her eyes how much her father meant to her. I had to repeat that I couldn't promise he would come home, but I also promised I would do everything in my power to ensure that he did.

That bloody strategic planning! Couldn't it tell us something else?

No, it couldn't – not in light of the constant danger we would be in. The danger of losing not just a few, but many comrades.

On what basis could I make such a bleak and sweeping statement?

A strategy isn't designed to be filed away on a shelf; a strategy is something you live and breathe, day in and day out.

On the basis of the tough, exhausting and time-consuming strategic planning carried out by my staff. A strategy isn't designed to be filed away on a shelf; a strategy is something you live and breathe, day in and day out. It's not only absolutely essential in order to complete a task – whether in a military unit, a company or local government – but it's also crucial for you, as a leader, to be able to live with yourself for the rest of your life.

To live with yourself for the rest of your life. Can a strategy really offer you that kind of peace? And what characterises a good strategy anyway?

If something goes wrong in your organisation, you have to know that you made all the preparations you possibly could, considered every thought and idea, and that you worked out your plan of action after having posed all the relevant questions.

For me personally, continually working on the strategy meant that I became increasingly aware of the demands that would be placed on me as a leader. The military decision-making process we were using is, in my opinion, excellent in many ways, and superior to the models used in industry, at business schools and consultancies. More on that later.

The disadvantage with the military model is that it takes an incredibly long time to learn, and possibly several years before it becomes second nature. But once you've learned how to get the most out of this model, you'll find it can carry you through the greatest and most difficult challenges.

When, using the model, we had analysed the situation and determined that we did indeed have to take an offensive role, we set about gathering as much information as we could about the Taliban's abilities, capacities, strengths and weaknesses, looking critically and soberly at our own. This may resemble many other plans, but what's special about the military model is that you spend a lot of time on war gaming – on confrontations between yourself and the enemy, opponent or competitor. I'll give a more thorough introduction to this model later in the chapter.

The point is that throughout the process you must be honest with your employees and everybody else involved, making sure they are aware of the potential consequences in advance and that they have the opportunity to prepare themselves. After the war, I met the bereaved relatives of the soldiers who had been killed. I needed to know, so that I could tell them, why their loved-ones had died and what it was we were trying to achieve. As the soldiers' commanding officer, for me it was crucial that the strategy we developed, and which served as the foundation of all our activities in Helmand, was so carefully thought-through that it would be an asset both before and after the mission. Plans were adjusted and corrected frequently, but the fundamental elements remained in place.

The strategy gave me peace of mind. When I spoke to the daughter in Varde (thankfully her father made it home, physically and mentally unscathed), or when I spoke to the loved-ones of fallen soldiers after the mission, I knew I could fall back on the thousands of calculations that myself and my staff had made. This sense of calm meant that I could be there for the bereaved. I had always taken a clear stance, both before we left and during the mission, and I could also be true to myself when we came home.

I'm not saying that it was a great comfort to the relatives to know we had a clear strategy. They had lost someone incredibly precious to them, and not even the best strategy could change that. But I think I was able to better support them when it came to discussing what had actually happened in Helmand, and why it had happened. And for me, personally, it was of the utmost importance that our work on the strategy was so thorough – otherwise I would have found it difficult to live with myself in the years afterwards.

In the months before our deployment to Helmand, we managed to weigh up every single scenario and every single challenge – not just in relation to the Taliban, but also to the soldiers' loved-ones and the press. How would we cope with relatives on the home front becoming worried and afraid? What would we do when soldiers were killed or injured? How would we proceed? What would we do if we faced criticism in the press?

Everything was painstakingly analysed, but it was worth all the effort: it meant that we were never blindsided by something we hadn't foreseen and mentally prepared for. We were vastly quicker to act and often able to keep one step ahead. The Taliban were a terrible opponent, one that demanded a particularly strong strategy.

We knew that in order to have any chance of ridding Gereshk and the Green Zone of the Taliban – or at least of making progress in the area possible – we had to always be one step ahead of them. This meant we needed to mentally prepare ourselves in the run-up to the offensive operations, in the knowledge that we wouldn't all make it home to Denmark. We knew we would lose some of our comrades and that there was no guarantee we'd come home ourselves.

With these thoughts at the back of my mind, I had to make sure everyone was prepared for the fact that there would be no let-up during the mission: the Taliban doesn't allow you time to take a breather. We simply had to accomplish what we set out to do, regardless of whether we were attacked or lost fellow soldiers.

This is why I started using the phrase, 'tomorrow we attack again'. By this, I meant that no matter how hard we were hit, we would look each other in the eyes and say, 'today we grieve for the fallen, but tomorrow we attack again'.

At first this might well be perceived as a little macho, but it wasn't intended as a soundbite. It was a necessary approach because, after going through the process of forming a strategy, we were aware of the consequences of not keeping up the pressure on the Taliban. If we allowed them to choose the time and place of every confrontation, we would suffer serious losses.

The British company we relieved on the front line, fighting the Taliban, could attest to that. There were initially 120 soldiers, mostly in stationary positions, which meant that they were repeatedly attacked. When we arrived in the area, there were only around fifty soldiers still fighting. It was a frustrating sight, and a harsh reminder of the challenge we were facing.

Nine of the company's soldiers had been killed, and seventeen were severely wounded. A large number were injured to the point where they could no longer take part in operations. Moreover, the large town of Gereshk was fully controlled by the Taliban. It seemed like a ghost town when we arrived, and two weeks before we moved in it had been rocked by a massive explosion. On 10 September 2007 a suicide bomber had set off a large bomb in the middle of the market square. Twenty-six people were killed, and more than thirty received serious injuries.

The strategy we had prepared was about to be tested. We had to tell ourselves that if we were reactive and passive, we would be hit hard – again and again and again. If we wanted to put the Taliban on the retreat, and bring as many of our soldiers as possible home again, we had to go on the offensive.

It has been my experience that strategic planning is rarely accorded the serious significance and appreciation it deserves, either in business or elsewhere. Many people underestimate the degree of depth required. Often, they approach this kind of planning in a haphazard, superficial and unstructured manner, lacking the analytical tools they need.

The problem is that if you allocate too few resources to developing your business strategy, you will end up focusing too much on the short-term, you won't bring out the best in your employees, and you will risk becoming too reactive and slow in comparison to your competitors – all because you didn't do a bit of extra spadework, which would have answered a whole host of questions. Your strategy will be superficial, and end up being shelved alongside all the previous ones.

In the military, the first step is always to define your enemies by garnering as much information about them as possible, and familiarise yourself with their strengths and weaknesses.

Several years ago, together with some good friends from the business and research communities, I developed a course on strategy. In it we attempted to bring together the best features of the military's analytical and organisational toolkit, combining them with the best tools from the worlds of industry and research, in order to provide support for businesses' strategic development. We ran the course for large and medium-sized companies, a few organisations and a local authority, before my new job as Master of Ceremonies meant I had to call a halt.

It would be too much of a detour to go into detail about the content of the course, but fundamentally it was about forcing senior management to dig deep and get to know both their own company and the competition back to front. We drew particular inspiration from war gaming, which is an important tool in military strategic planning and a permanent part of all combat estimates.

In the military, the first step is always to define your enemies by garnering as much information about them as possible, and familiarise yourself with their strengths and weaknesses. In industry, 'enemies' naturally translates to 'competitors', or simply a picture of the challenges ahead.

On a typical course, we identify a company's most important competitors, then selected employees are given at least a week to analyse them in great detail – their products, finances, staff, media strategy, international profile and much more. I have worked with some companies where their competitors were judged to be so strong that they had the potential to shut down the company. There was a general feeling of 'us or them'.

In the phase leading up to the weekend we were meeting, we also pinpointed the five or six parameters that would be crucial for the company's success – whether it would sink or swim in the marketplace – focusing on, for instance, product development, branding, communication or financial health.

The strategy course would then be conducted over the weekend, and at the most fundamental level it was about confronting the company's management with every single competitor for every single parameter. The competitors were represented by the employees who had spent a whole week preparing, and by this point knew everything worth knowing about their subject.

The company's own management – in practice, the managing director – was compelled to present a plan, i.e. to act, then the competitors would respond, the managing director would again react and the competitors respond in their turn. Provisional conclusions were drawn at every stage of the confrontation. The process followed a fixed pattern: action, reaction, action, reaction, provisional conclusion. Then we started over with a new competitor or a new parameter.

Many hours later, all the relevant issues had been addressed, and the management were able to draw a general conclusion about what the key points within a new strategy should be. Where was there an opportunity to improve the business and keep the company one step ahead of the competition?

Sometimes it was blindingly obvious where the company should bring its weight to bear and – to use a military expression – employ focused violence to win the 'war'. On other occasions the picture was murkier, with additional time required to focus on three or four areas. In all cases, it was a difficult and time-consuming process, demanding a referee (me) who could guide the interactions between the managing director and the competitors. The end result was always a high degree of strategic clarity and a number of provisional conclusions, which the company could use going forward.

We spent, on average, six hours on this concentrated confrontation, and afterwards it was always clear that the director was completely and utterly exhausted. It was, however, just as clear that once we had drawn all these various conclusions about the strengths and weaknesses of the company in comparison with its competitors, the subsequent stages of the process were a source of great inspiration.

Here, as a 'referee', I could take a step back and simply facilitate the discussions going on among the management. In light of the knowledge now shared by everyone in the room, the areas where further work was needed could be properly addressed.

> The management are often eager to skip over a banal but immensely important question – 'What are we trying to achieve?'

When a military commander and his organisational staff carry out a similar execise, all possible areas of confrontation will have been covered by the time the battle commences, and throughout the process he will be briefed by his closest officers: 'We are now reaching decision point A. You need to be aware that we may be affected by ... You have the following options, should this occur ...'. This is how it works in practice. This is how you prepare for war. And this is how you make sure you're in a position to act quickly.

In my work with businesses and organisations on strategy and leadership, I have noticed something else, too: the management are often eager to skip over a banal but immensely important question – 'What are we trying to achieve?' Or, more precisely: 'Why are we here?'

'Why' is a question that must be asked many times before you get to the heart of the matter. Let me give you an example:

A Scandinavian firm with around 500 employees that specialised in creating experiences and development opportunities for clients was facing a particular challenge: to retain their best members of staff. On the strategy course it emerged that many of the managers actually found it rather difficult to put the overall mission of the company into words. They couldn't tell you why they did what they did.

On one level, of course, their mission was to create experiences for clients. But why? Well, to earn money for the owners, so that the firm could continue to grow. But again: why?

By insisting on asking the question again and again, you gradually boil things down to the nitty-gritty. It emerged that the Scandinavian company didn't have a proper strategy that the managers could identify with. Promoting growth is all very well, and obviously it made their numbers look great, but to what purpose? They lacked a more fundamental vision.

Using this process, they established that the underlying reason for their existence was to connect people with each other, giving them experiences that would enable them to develop together. And once the managers and employees had a strategy they could identify with, it became much easier to put the business's DNA into words. After a few more 'whys', they were able to present a higher objective still, which was about building networks and cross-border relationships, promoting cultural understanding, and creating better and safer products – it now seemed as if there were virtually no limits to how much the company could contribute to the world.

Many other issues were also brought to light. The most important one being that this higher goal wasn't just about protecting the company's bottom line. It had deeper significance. And it was incredibly important for the employees to dig a little deeper into the business, understanding its culture and identity.

In my experience, you need to ask the same irritating question – 'why?' – two, three, maybe even four times before you reach your justification for existence: why are we really here? What is our mission? What are our ethical standards and values?

Once you have an answer to that question, it means you have finally identified the essentials, right at the heart of the company. This is a place of camaraderie, and you then have a much better basis from which to recruit and retain the most talented managers and employees. Once everybody understands why they do what they do, it's easier to take pride in working for the company, and to enjoy it. As an employee, it's simple to explain to people – your grandma, for instance, when she asks at a family get-together – why you'd rather work for that company than any other.

When you understand the essentials, you also have a better opportunity to work 'in the spirit of the company'. You can act and be proactive when it is expected and necessary. If you don't have an underlying understanding of what you're doing, you often end up doing nothing at all.

So if, as a manager, you feel irritated that your employ-ees aren't acting in what you perceive to be the right way, you should begin by asking yourself whether they actually have the knowledge and motivation required to do so.

Presenting your strategy in front of everybody is an abso-lutely crucial exercise. It's not easy, because you may need to present it to various groups of people in different ways. The importance of how you communicate must not be underestimated. But as a general rule, it's best when a leader simply gets up onto a soapbox and presents their strategy through words, gestures and sheer passion. Don't expect your employees to read about it on the intranet. The strategy must be lived, discussed and adjusted.

My message is this: a company must know itself, and should communicate this knowledge to everybody within the organisation, so that they don't just understand but actually feel the strategy. When this succeeds, the result is a proactive organisation that will most likely stay one step ahead of the competition.

In Helmand, my units were spread over a wide area, so I couldn't be nearby all the time. The leader on the ground always had to act with the overarching strategy in mind – in other words, needed to understand the spirit and inten-tion of the overall plan.

In a military context, there is always an intention asso-ciated with the mission. You are given an assignment or goal to be achieved, followed by a sentence that explains the reasoning behind it: 'You are to attack the area around X in order to lay the groundwork for Y.'

In Helmand, the overall objective and intention behind our operations was always to lay the groundwork that would enable the Afghan people to return to their homes, and provide them with a basic level of safety, while setting the process of development and rebuilding in motion.

This was also the essence of the Commander's Intent, which I formulated in a one-and-a-half-page document before our deployment. Brief and to-the-point, it spelled out the purpose of our presence in Afghanistan. It emphasised the difficulty of the mission – after all, there wasn't much chance of persuading the Taliban to leave the area. Our assignment necessitated a military offensive, which meant that we had to take the initiative in all respects, never allowing ourselves to become simply reactive. And it made clear the fact that all our operations would take place on conscientious and ethically defensible terms. Above all, we would do our utmost to avoid civilian casualties.

In wartime you have to expect the unexpected. You only stick to the plan until you first make contact with the enemy – after that, you have to act in the now. You realise that you can't carry out the assignment in the way you planned, but if you keep your intention and goal in mind, your colleagues will work out an alternative way to get the job done.

This mentality is an integral part of the way we train Danish soldiers. Even the youngest squaddie learns how to take the initiative and act while keeping the overall goal in mind, and it is precisely this that has earned the Danish army international renown.

So, what pitfalls should you be aware of when working out a unique strategy? I have already mentioned a few: a lack of appreciation of how deep you have to dig, and the importance of thoroughly integrating the strategy throughout the organisation. It requires patience, willpower and persistence. You have to be insistent about following up on the plan, keeping an eye on how it develops and discussing progress. Frankly, you need a war room, with employees who can help the management to focus on the next decision point.

If the strategy simply ends up in a ring-binder on a shelf somewhere, then fundamentally, it has been one giant waste of time.

As far as I'm concerned, the biggest danger is that the management is invisible and disengaged, leaving all the actual work to consultants.

As far as I'm concerned, the biggest danger is that the management is invisible and disengaged, leaving all the actual work to consultants. When a consultancy firm takes on the task of developing a strategy – in the context of a larger turnaround or major cutbacks, for instance – employees begin to lose faith in their own management. As a consequence, the company can end up losing their most talented people, the spirit of solidarity among the staff takes a nosedive and their sense of identity crumbles.

In the situations where I have worked as a consultant with private businesses, I have tried to be vigilant about falling into exactly this trap. They cannot simply 'outsource' responsibility to me. Consultants aren't God's gift to humanity. It isn't their job to come up with the perfect solution. They are simply there to facilitate the process and inspire the management to look towards a new future.

I have no doubt that consultants and consultancy firms will generally be in agreement on this. Rather, it is senior management across various businesses, organisations and local authorities who need to be aware of the problem.

The management should take their time defining what exactly it is that the consultants are there to do, and what structures and underlying factors they need to take into account. If, then, the consultants launch into their analyses with little regard for these fundamental requirements, the management will quickly lose support among the company's own ranks, and this can be fatal.

To take a hypothetical example: let's say Cristiano Ronaldo and Lionel Messi discovered that consultants were arriving at Real Madrid or FC Barcelona to explore the possibility of making efficiency improvements. One non-negotiable requirement would be for the consultants to respect the fact that professional footballers need medical care – personal trainers, doctors, physiotherapists and massage therapists. If the players found that the clubs were planning to make cuts in that area on the basis of a consultant's report, no amount of money would be enough to compensate for the gaffe.

It would be an attack on the players' professional identity, which rests on such concepts as strength and robustness. If you start picking at employees' sense of identity in order to make a short-sighted cutback, you can find yourself with far more serious consequences on your hands – ultimately, in my hypothetical case, it might mean that Messi and Ronaldo would quite literally hang up their boots at the club.

My message is clear. A leader must be endlessly vigilant in making sure that consultants are purely a source of support and inspiration. Let me hammer this point home: it has to be the management itself behind the wheel, steering the company through the process and ensuring that the issues key to its identity are understood and respected.

To summarise: as mentioned earlier, we need something to stand up for if we want to excel. In my world, this something is often integral to the company's vision and strategy. It is worked out in a purposeful and deliberate manner, through hard graft. And everyone – both employees and managers – must be able to feel it in their day-to-day working lives.

As the head of a company, organisation or local authority, a strategy will prove invaluable the day misfortune strikes. In working on the plan, you will have identified potential dangers, giving yourself a mental head start – and you may even have a procedure already in place so that you and your employees know what to expect in those circumstances. You will have managers and employees who dare to go first.

Your strategy will, however, require follow-up work, training and professional development. In the next chapter, I will share my experiences in these areas. This follow up takes place in light of the framework and issues identified by the strategy. It's then time to start filling in the blanks through training and development (chapter 3) and by recruiting employees who are up to the task (chapter 4).

Train Like You Fight

'YOU SHOULDN'T run in the camp, chaplain. It makes the soldiers uneasy.'

That was my spontaneous reaction when I saw our chaplain come rushing towards me and my second-in-command one day in October 2007. We were together, for once, at headquarters in Camp Bastion, discussing our strategy for the coming months. But I could soon see from the chaplain's serious and concerned expression that there was a reason he was running.

'We've got a T1. It's the head. It's Anders Storrud!'

When a wounded soldier is categorised as a T1, you know his injuries are life-threatening.

'That can't be right, it *mustn't* be right,' was my first thought, as we all ran towards the tactical operations centre. But it was. Anders' condition was *extremely* serious.

That day, he and his company had been in the midst of an operation against the Taliban in the Green Zone. Its name was Operation Venus, and its goal was to destroy a mortar unit that could fire shells at our troops. Taking into account various observations, measurements and intelligence information, we had an accurate idea of where the mortar was positioned. At the same time as the specific attack on the mortar, we were also targeting several other enemy positions, trying to force the Taliban further up into the valley and away from the town of Gereshk.

On 15 October at 09:25, Company Commander Anders Storrud gave the order: 'Move, move!' Shortly afterwards, our experts in electronic warfare were able to tell us that the Taliban were communicating about our company's movements in the valley and so, when the first houses were searched, there was no trace of the mortar. It had already been removed.

Anders was in an armoured personnel carrier on the plateau above the valley, from which he could observe the soldiers' movements. Moving around within the area was incredibly time-consuming, so it was only at approximately 2pm that he took the decision to withdraw the units, after a day where – against expectations – there had been no fighting.

Anders remained in his command vehicle on the desert plateau to ensure his soldiers' safety as they drew back, standing up to get a better overview. As they neared the gathering point, there was a sudden, violent bang, followed by several others. Clearly, the Taliban had been waiting until the soldiers withdrew before launching a mortar attack.

The last impact proved disastrous, landing only three metres from Anders' armoured vehicle. One of the soldiers in the personnel carrier told us later that he felt a hard blow to his left forearm as a fragment of the shell penetrated it, slicing through a nerve. The driver, who had known Anders for many years and fought alongside him on many international missions, turned around to make sure everything was ok. The first thing he noticed was that his commanding officer had fallen down into the vehicle. Anders Storrud had been struck in the head by a fragment of the shell – bleeding profusely from the mouth and cheek, he had lost consciousness.

It was clear to everyone in the vehicle that the situation was dire. They immediately requested a helicopter evacuation. Anders needed to be taken to the field hospital as soon as possible.

Other people were listening over the radio and, on hearing the service number read out from Anders' uniform as emergency medical care was called in, realised that the casualty wasn't a young soldier but someone older and more senior. This narrowed the field considerably – after all, the unit was deployed on the front lines against the Taliban, so the average age for a soldier on active duty wasn't particularly high. Some of them began to feel uneasy. They also noticed that they could no longer hear Anders' voice over the radio.

The company soon became aware that it was, indeed, their commanding officer who had received a life-threatening injury. It was hard to accept. Yes, he'd been hit and was on his way to the field hospital, but his soldiers thought he'd pull through. And he'd be back. If they had to, they were ready to carry or drive him round. After all, this was Anders!

I immediately decided that I and my bodyguard Christian would fly out to Sandford, the company's camp in the desert. A Chinook helicopter was requisitioned. Just as we were taking off from Camp Bastion, the helicopter carrying Anders landed next to us. Many thoughts were rushing through my head as we flew to Sandford.

'He'll survive. Of course he will,' I thought, but I also had to prepare myself for the possibility that the company I was on my way to meet might lose its commanding officer.

Who would take charge of the company now? It would naturally have been Anders' second-in-command, but he had just returned to Denmark because of a serious illness in the family, leaving the company with neither a commanding officer nor a second-in-command at a time when its soldiers were up against some of the fiercest fighting a Danish unit had experienced in living memory.

When I arrived at the desert base of Sandford, the first thing I did was check the crew in Anders' vehicle. I knew them all well. They were deeply affected, but – incredibly – they were calm enough to talk about the situation. Like the rest of us, they were firmly convinced that Anders would pull through.

Then I gathered the whole company together and told them what I knew: 'Anders is seriously wounded, but he's currently being treated and they will make every effort to save him.' I also said that they would be continuously updated on his progress, and would receive further information as soon as I had word from my second-in-command, Mads Rahbek, via our satellite phone.

Mads and I were in close contact. The prognosis teetered back and forth, but even at its most optimistic it offered little hope that Anders would return to the company in the foreseeable future. Once that became clear, I was faced with an inevitable decision: I had to choose one person from among three excellent platoon commanders and ask him to take charge of the whole company. In other words, he had to be ready to jump two rungs up the ladder.

The platoon commander was chosen and informed. With immediate effect, Mads Mikkelsen became responsible for a company that had lost two of its members within three weeks and seen five badly injured. His own second-in-command had been seriously wounded the previous week when his car hit a roadside bomb, so in Mads Mikkelsen's own unit a young sergeant also had to be willing to leap two levels up and take charge of a whole platoon.

You lose people during wartime, but the mission must be completed. It doesn't just disappear. So you always have to be ready to take on another leader's duties. It's a fact that's callous and incredibly demanding, but unavoidable. Once the decision had been made and Mads knew it was his responsibility to see through the rest of the mission over the next few days, we sat down to talk things through.

You lose people during wartime, but the mission must be completed. It doesn't just disappear. So you always have to be ready to take on another leader's duties.

Mads was deeply affected by the situation, as we all were, but he was also extremely professional. He knew, for instance, that it would be dangerous to stop patrolling the area for a few days, because it would give the Taliban a chance to regroup, prepare more ambushes and intimidate the locals. No – the mission went on, and it had to be carried out.

In fact, this was helpful for Mads. We neither could nor should proceed any other way, even though the company commander was lying in a field hospital with life-threatening injuries. The mission had to remain the primary focus. Was it tough? Yes. Was it necessary? Yes.

I chatted to Mads about what he had learned at the military academy and on international missions in Kosovo and elsewhere. I had to be sure that he understood the larger framework of which the company was a part. The other units around him were engaged in all sorts of different operations. It was a great relief to find that Mads fully understood the company's role within this bigger campaign. Seeing him leap two rungs up the ladder with such speed, composure and self-possession, to take ownership of his new role as company commander was, for me, a confirmation of the quality of our training in the Danish armed forces. We now found ourselves in a situation exactly like the ones Mads, and many other officers, had been trained for at the academy.

You always have to be trained at two levels above your current position. You have to know what it is you're part of so that you can act in accordance with the concerns and intentions devised by those in more senior roles. If necessary, you should be able to assume a leadership role at a level above your own. This was the mantra drummed into us during our training, and now it was unfolding in reality.

Mads knew that he was up to the task. Like the other two platoon commanders, he was ready to take charge. I told him I would remain with the company for as long as he wanted, and I could tell

You always have to be trained at two levels above your current position. You have to know what it is you're part of so that you can act in accordance with the concerns and intentions devised by those in more senior roles.

he was glad to have the support, but I also emphasised that I wasn't the *de facto* head of the company. He was.

Anders' condition worsened as the evening went on. My thoughts were with the company, but they were also with his loved-ones in Denmark. I knew that Anders' wife was being contacted by my own commanding officer in Denmark, the commander of the Royal Lifeguards, Colonel Lasse Harkjær.

I also had to gather my composure on a more personal level, as it was my youngest son's birthday and I had promised to call home via the satellite phone. Kristoffer was turning twelve, and everybody knows that birthdays are important at that age.

He chatted merrily away about what a good day he had had, then finally asked if I was ok too. What could I say? I told him, 'Daddy's fine ...'.

When my wife came on the line, she could immediately tell from my voice that something was amiss. Nothing had appeared in the media, but I had to prepare Tine for the fact that before long she might hear some 'breaking news'. We didn't know what the press would say, but it might be something along the lines of 'Danish commander fatally wounded in Helmand'.

I told Tine – although obviously she could work it out for herself – that it wasn't me who had been injured, but Anders. Tine went quiet. She cried, then had to go back to the birthday party unable to tell anybody what was wrong.

On the morning of 16 October, it became clear that Anders couldn't be saved. For a while we hoped he could at least be flown back home to Denmark so that his family could say goodbye, but eventually the doctors had to give up on this too. Once all hope was gone, they removed the tubes and other medical equipment that was keeping him artificially alive.

I was standing by myself in a corner of Forward Operating Base Sandford when I got the call. Mads Rahbek, my second-in-command, said:

'Kim, I'm incredibly sorry to have to tell you this, but Anders passed away at 10:59. I held his hand as he slipped away.'

I couldn't speak. I just crouched down and made sure no one at the base could see me. Mads could hear me sobbing. 'Are you ok?' he asked. After a moment, I was able to answer: 'Yes, Mads, I'm ok. I'm just so very, very sorry.'

I had been expecting the news, but it still hit me extremely hard. Much harder than I had realised or braced myself for.

Once I had recovered, I needed to prepare myself to gather the company and give the most difficult speech I have ever had to make. All the soldiers had been hoping for a miracle; perhaps we even felt convinced that one would happen. Now I had to tell them that Anders was dead. During wartime, officers always have to be prepared to lose their lives. It's second nature for an officer to end every order with the words: 'If I get killed, you should ..., keep your focus on ..., stop ...'. We officers know that the job has got to be done, and we make every effort to ensure that it is done, even when times are at their most bleak. Completing the mission takes priority.

My speech to the company (during which I had to pause several times) had the following message:

'If Anders were here now, he would tell us to continue with the mission. To keep putting pressure on the Taliban, to not let ourselves break, to try and create a better environment for ordinary Afghans. The sun rises and it sets. Today has been a long, hard and incredibly sad day. Tomorrow the sun will rise again, and it will be a good day. A day where we keep creating more opportunities for the Afghan people. That's what Anders would have wanted. Tomorrow we attack again!'

Three killed, five badly wounded and many other soldiers hurt. How could the unit continue fighting just one day later, risking losing more of its members? How could so many leaders move up the ranks and continue to fulfil their duties with extraordinary professionalism, trusted by the soldiers and still believing in themselves?

The answer lies in their training. The training that myself and my officers received was centred, as I mentioned earlier, around always being capable of understanding and acting 'two levels up and two levels down'.

The officer's training we were given can best be described as an academicised kind of hands-on apprenticeship, but a hands-on apprenticeship nonetheless. What does that mean in practice? Fundamentally, it means that every general has at some point been an ordinary soldier.

Moving up the ranks before finally becoming a general gives you a solid understanding of the levels 'below you', especially if you don't forget where you came from on the way up. Being familiar with the lower levels of the army's hierarchically structured system is a natural part of military life.

But what about the levels above you? It requires a deliberate training philosophy to maintain a constant focus on understanding and being familiar with them, too. I have personally experienced this kind of deliberate training, and it was immensely rewarding – not only in terms of my job in the armed forces, but also for my work in industry, at embassies and at the royal court.

Employees who can act swiftly, and in accordance with the overall intentions of the management, are an enormous asset to any organisation. Most people agree on that. When I attended the military academy as a young man, I learned about the role I was intended to fulfil. This was initially as a platoon commander with responsibility for thirty men. But alongside this training they put a lot of resources towards training me to understand how to lead a company of 150 soldiers and a battalion of over 500 soldiers. Each level has its own inherent complications. The more people you have to be able to lead, the more nuances there are.

Employees who can act swiftly, and in accordance with the overall intentions of the management, are an enormous asset to any organisation.

The same principle followed me later in my career. During my training to lead a battalion of over 500 soldiers, I was also taught to be capable of leading a brigade and – beyond that – a division of several thousand soldiers.

An increasingly comprehensive appreciation of the levels above me was therefore at the core of my training, which naturally meant that the larger the unit I was supposed to be able to lead, the greater the focus on political and international issues, civilian roles and the importance of communication and the media.

The final piece of training I received in the armed forces took place at the European Security and Defence College in Brussels. Here, I experienced teaching at the highest political and military strategic level.

This insight into levels higher up the organisation – or robustness, as we might also call it – meant that I found it easy to understand why my superiors pursued various assignments, going about reaching their goal in a particular way. At the same time, it was easy to see my own role within that.

It is precisely this appreciation for your superiors' intentions and objectives that is crucial to success. This was also my experience as a battalion commander in Helmand. When we lost radio contact, when something went wrong or the plan had to be rethought without reference to my own British commander, I always had a clear sense of how his mind worked. I thought: 'What would Brigadier John Lorimer say if he were standing in front of me?' I was never in doubt as to the answer.

This understanding was vital in order to be capable of making independent decisions. I was rarely able to wait for clear directives, and neither were the officers working below me. The whole way down the hierarchy, an appreciation of our overall strategy, vision and purpose was of crucial significance.

If, as a leader, you expect your commanders to be able to act with you in mind, you must first ask yourself whether they have the training necessary to do so.

That's all very well, but you can't do the same thing in the private sector or somewhere like that, I often hear. But that's not true. I have witnessed a similar approach in many businesses.

As an example of a corporation that thinks along the same lines, I can give the global Danish transport and logistics company DSV, which is known for making sure its managers understand what life is like for drivers by having the directors and other senior figures accompany them on their journeys across Europe.

If, as a leader, you expect your commanders to be able to act with you in mind, you must first ask yourself whether they have the training necessary to do so.

A Danish supermarket chain I have worked with has a philosophy whereby the managers in the individual shops are able to act with a high degree of independence. During their training, they are taught, in great detail, about the chain's approach to human resources, customer service, media relations, competitors and so on.

It's always sensible to ask yourself whether you are sure that your employees' level of knowledge is sufficient for them to be able to jump up a level without any fuss, should the need arise.

At the royal court, we have been training employees for many years to ensure that the whole organisation can act quickly and appropriately in any situation. Competency profiles are worked up on every single employee. Five levels are defined within each area of competence, which can be used to create an appreciation of the whole. There are professional development days, where different divisions and levels interact. Each department has made a short video presentation that new employees can watch when they begin at the royal court, so that from the outset they get a sense of the organisation and the work that needs to be done.

From my perspective, the aim is that, as an employee, you need to be familiar with what the people above, below and either side of you actually need, and only when you understand this can you contribute. Taken as a whole, it produces a powerful overall sense of cohesion. But it doesn't happen of its own accord. It requires training.

At the same time, it is important to remain focused on the people who have to perform at the highest level out on the front lines. It might be a cashier, a soldier, the queen's chauffeur or an employee at the ambassador's consulate: wherever a 'customer' is being served, the business is being measured and judged. Every day. So everybody must be in a position to support the levels closest to 'the front'. It's also healthy to bear that in mind when you're thinking two levels up and two levels down within a company.

If you're going to train like you fight – to return to the world of military terminology – you also have to look at structures and environments. A leader's environment is often beset by chaos and uncertainty, therefore, an ability to 'love the chaos' is a non-negotiable requirement.

That's not something most people embrace. If we find ourselves in a chaotic situation, most of us will try to extricate ourselves from it as soon as possible. But leadership in a chaotic environment is simply part of everyday life for a leader on the front lines. A leader who can't command or act amidst chaos isn't much good when it comes to the crunch.

A leader's environment is often beset by chaos and uncertainty, therefore, an ability to 'love the chaos' is a non-negotiable requirement.

This is why you require training on how to lead in chaotic circumstances – and it needs to be repeated. Chaos, when you need to make quick decisions, often under fire, demands training, training and more training. Again, let me emphasise, leaders who can act under those conditions aren't automatically found in the halls of academia. As officers, we were given an academic perspective – which is absolutely necessary – but we were also given intensive hands-on training during exercises, in the cold and extreme heat, with the sands of the desert in our mouths, throats and eyes. This is where practical leaders are formed, ones who can thrive in chaos.

Try to spend a minute or two thinking about your own situation at work. Are there occasions when you have to perform as a leader under tight time constraints and maybe even in a chaotic situation? I think all leaders have experienced that to a certain extent. The difference is that I and my officers were given extremely focused training before

80

we were deployed, which prepared us to lead in a chaotic environment. Were you?

'Shall we go over it again?' I heard this question countless times before I experienced actual combat. My answer was usually that it was important for our procedures to become second nature, so that as soldiers we would never be in any doubt as to how to act in the heat of battle. But I didn't know that – it was an article of faith rather than knowledge.

That's no longer the case. After the first bout of intense fighting, where chaos reigned, the reports from the soldiers on the front lines were full of astonishment: 'That was exactly like we practised all those times.'

The soldiers discovered that their training allowed the unit to act quickly and with pinpoint precision, despite the utter chaos of their environment. It gave them a profound sense of calm. All those exercises actually worked in practice.

The Centre for Military Physical Training was the first place in the world to begin measuring our soldiers' physical condition when they were deployed – including in active operations – in Helmand. The measurements spoke louder than words. Simply getting ready for patrols in the verdant Green Zone in Helmand, carrying a heavy weight on your back and shoulders, resulted in a pulse so high that simply maintaining concentration was a challenge.

When this was combined with a significant loss of fluids as the hours passed, and a high degree of uncertainty followed by sudden outbreaks of fighting, the answer was unambiguous: in situations like that, soldiers can only act reflexively. You get tunnel vision, and when everything dissolves into chaos you have nothing to rely on but the procedures ingrained in your muscle memory.

I felt that all those years of pushing, prodding and preaching at soldiers to rehearse again and again was necessary, but I didn't know that for sure. It was an 'aha' moment for me and my soldiers to be faced with the proof that you had to train as hard as humanly possible before you entered into combat. In the heat of battle, you have nothing but your training to fall back on. You act reflexively, relying on muscle memory. Your training is your lifeline.

It also requires a profound recognition that you are simply one person among many. Every single soldier is vital if you want to return home as a group, platoon or company. You should train together so often that you all become part of a well-oiled machine, working in synch. If one of your fellow soldiers is ill or absent, the whole unit pays the price.

Does this sound naïve? Didn't we know that already? No! We had an idea of it, but we had to actually *learn* it the hard way. The lessons in places like Iraq and Afghanistan have left their mark on all the leaders involved. Respect for the kind of preparation that enables you to handle chaos is now imprinted in every officer responsible for training.

I am often asked how this military philosophy of training at least as hard as you fight can be translated into reality in, for instance, industry or local government.

The question surprises me because, on the face of it, it seems easy to 'translate'. Once you have your strategy, and therefore also your precise objectives in place, it's time to establish a training plan for your staff. Ask yourself a few important questions: what should be our particular focus? What will that mean for the employees who contribute towards realising those objectives?

If your ambition is to improve all your processes while combining that with increased speed in the key areas you've just defined, it's obvious that many elements of that can be trained, ingrained and will become second nature.

Essentially, if you really want to excel under pressure, the watchwords are training, training and more training. In the world of sports, everybody understands that. It seems obvious for the police or for people working on an oil rig in the middle of the sea, too. But my claim is that intensive training, and courses that focus on being able to act quickly and appropriately in core areas, is the key to creating good results in all kinds of organisations.

Essentially, if you really want to excel under pressure, the watchwords are training, training and more training.

The international construction company NCC showed me an example of strong leadership under chaotic circumstances, including the ability to make rapid decisions and the willingness to take responsibility, when at the end of 2014 I went on a leadership training course with the corporation's directors.

Just before the session, NCC had suffered an accident in which a building complex collapsed in Denmark. The corporation already had a plan of action in place for when (or if) a serious situation arose, which was now demonstrating its value. Everybody knew in advance who was supposed to do what, where, when and how. Via the Danish media they announced that NCC immediately took responsibility, even though they could have tried to shift the blame onto a sub-contractor. A director was on site immediately, explaining what was going to happen and what they intended to do next.

It was reassuring and engendered confidence, and afterwards they largely managed to avoid serious negative criticism in the media.

During my conversations with the senior managers, I got a deep insight into the deliberate approach the NCC took to leadership in chaotic situations. When an accident occurred, they immediately stepped forward to take responsibility, act on the situation and follow up. The leaders, who were clearly identified in any given situation, found themselves on the front lines at ultra-short notice.

There wasn't time to discuss all the details of the incident with their headquarters in Stockholm, but they didn't need to: the managers on the scene had been properly prepared, so they had a sense for, and understanding of, the corporation's policy when it came to accidents like the one that had taken place.

In chaotic situations, it can sometimes be necessary – even vital – to take a series of quick 80% optimal decisions, instead of trying to find a single 100% perfect one. The latter would obviously be ideal, but if it comes too late it's not going to be much help.

This issue, too, necessitates a particular focus on the leaders chosen. I have met many managers who can only work in terms of optimal situations. They're unable to drag themselves away from trying to find a 100% perfect solution, which means that it's a bad idea to put them on the front lines during wartime; at the front you can never, in reality, find a solution that's 100% optimal.

On the other hand, we'd all be a little worried if an eye surgeon announced just before a retina operation that he was actually quite happy with solutions that were 80% perfect. My point is that different situations demand different kinds of leadership. We need to be capable of distinguishing between the type of leader who thrives in chaos and the kind of leader who cannot function in it. One hundred per cent is always the best solution, but if it's impossible under the given circumstances, a leader must be able to prioritise and make choices.

All in all, it is in an understanding of how things work 'two levels up and two levels down', and in the mastery of leadership under chaotic circumstances, that I have witnessed excellence in leadership. Managers who have understood the greater whole of which they are a part, and who can act proactively, get results. If they also radiate the calm needed to guide their ship safely to harbour, despite the chaos around them, then they can count on the support of their employees.

The word *leadership* seems appropriate in this regard: as a leader you are like the captain of a ship, steering a course through dangerous rocks and reefs as a storm rages around you.

The highest levels of performance are achieved by independent managers who have the courage to lead with no need for minute-by-minute directives from above. Many people think, as discussed earlier, that leadership in the military is about rigid, unyielding discipline. Nothing could be further from the truth.

The highest levels of performance are achieved by independent managers who have the courage to lead with no need for minute-by-minute directives from above.

Officers deployed on the front lines have to be incredibly creative and innovative in finding new solutions – all the time. They must possess great courage and a good deal of imagination, and that's not compatible with an inflexible approach. They involve their most talented soldiers in their deliberations, and only then do they make a decision.

This demands significant investment in leaders and leadership training. There are no shortcuts – leadership has always been a complex thing – so not even the most ingenious system of checks and balances, or the most sophisticated structures, guidelines and measurements, will ensure excellent management. After all, we're dealing with people, not robots.

We have to find and shape leaders who are brave enough to act according to the framework mapped out by senior management – whether that's in the form of political directives, the board's strategy and plan of action, the headteacher's timetables or the Lord Chamberlain's annual plan.

Even the worst framework for supervision and performance appraisals can be turned into something positive by a strong leader, and even the most rigorously thought-through plan is no guarantee of success if a manager is weak.

Everything depends on the leader, who has to be front and centre. The leader must have our attention.

This is why we need *leaders* to exercise leadership and *administrators* to administrate schedules, reports and key data. Every company requires both types of person, but must make sure they leave the staff to the leaders and the paperwork to the administrators.

Leaders were what I mainly needed in Helmand. Mads Mikkelsen and all the other soldiers who had to shift one or two rungs up the ladder – they were the kind of leaders who were willing to take responsibility, and they had the training to do exactly that.

During our deployment in Helmand, we were all given the opportunity to take some leave. This meant that we could go home to Denmark for two or three weeks – according to a schedule that had been worked out in advance – to spend time with our families and get some distance from Afghanistan (which, incidentally, wasn't easy to do).

We knew from the outset that the battalion commander, the company commanders, the platoon commanders and the section commanders would all be away for certain periods. This meant, of course, that everybody had to be prepared to take on a role that was different from their usual one.

All companies and organisations experience something equivalent. People go on holiday, they take time off in lieu of overtime, or they need to take sick leave. You can get ahead of this with a training program that ensures everybody is able to 'shift up', if necessary, as a matter of course.

Even if the need never arises, such training will still be beneficial, because everybody will be aware of how things work on the levels above them, and will be able to act on the basis of that knowledge.

Mads Mikkelsen, by the way, executed his duties brilliantly, managing to cope with the tremendous pressure on his shoulders until the second-in-command of the company returned from Denmark. If the unit had not had such a high level of training, the company would have been forced to stay on the base, look after itself and wait for an officer with the appropriate level of training to arrive. In reality, it successfully kept up the offensive against the Taliban.

Three years later, Mads was sent to Afghanistan again. Having undertaken further training at the Royal Danish Military Academy, where he was once more trained 'two levels up', he was made company commander. I know from close colleagues that, again, he excelled in this role. He knew how to be proactive, conducting himself in synch with his superior officers.

Having presented my thoughts about strategies and training, I want to devote the next chapter to assembling a team that can carry out that strategy.

One of my core messages in this book is that there is an integral connection between strategy, training and choosing the right people for the job. Before you begin the next chapter, think about whether this connection exists at your own company. Is your choice of employees the result of a carefully considered strategy? Or do things happen on an ad-hoc basis? Is your strategy adapted to the people in the company – or the other way around?

CHAPTER 4

Assemble a Dream Team

'THIS IS SO ANNOYING – I can't believe I made such an arrogant know-it-all part of the team. Why does he talk to his colleagues in such an abrasive and unpleasant way when they're actually asking perfectly sensible and relevant questions? Why can't he just be friendly?'

I was wondering exactly this during my days and nights deployed in northern Kosovo in 2005. Now at the rank of lieutenant colonel and serving as chief of staff with the Danish/French battalion, I was tasked with heading up the group of staff who worked out all the plans for our mission, supporting the battalion commander and the units on the ground. When the commander wasn't around, I had to be ready to take charge of the approximately 500 Danish and French soldiers in the battalion.

Our assignment was to keep the peace between the Kosovo Serbs and Kosovo Albanians in and around the city of Mitrovica. The situation was reasonably clear. We knew what scenarios to prepare ourselves for, and what problems might arise. This isn't to say that we were anticipating a mission without any particular challenges: we had to be constantly vigilant about the possibility of unrest, readying ourselves to deal with it. But it didn't seem likely that we would end up with a full-scale war on our hands.

So it was frankly irritating that not everybody on the team was able to recognise their place, support each other and avoid stirring up unnecessary internal strife. Hostilities between the Serbs and Albanians was one thing – after all, they were the reason we were in Kosovo in the first place – but friction between members of our own unit was quite another. It became an unnecessarily disruptive issue in my day-to-day activities.

Whose fault was that? It was wholly mine!

When it came time to assemble a team for the Kosovo mission, I decided not to alter the organisational structure we had spent many months building up. We'll take things as they come, I thought. I'm sure we'll be able to sort things out further down the line.

Deep down I knew we had a problem: one centrally placed officer had a tendency to undermine and irritate the unit. His approach to the units under our control was markedly arrogant. This arrogance was clearly rooted in his own ignorance of what was actually going on with them – of the challenges they faced and the support they needed. He was the person they were supposed to go to if they had problems, but he wasn't receptive to that. He thought he knew better than other people, and often remained committed to decisions even though they had no basis in reality. Moreover, his way of addressing people was unnecessarily abrasive, obviously creating a lot of frustration.

In an ideal world, this officer would never have come with us to Kosovo, but I nonetheless chose to include him. Why create conflict before we leave, I thought. I'm sure it will all be fine.

My last warning came from General Knud Bartels, at that time head of the Danish Division, who later became Chief of Defence and chair of NATO's military committee. During our last exercise before the mission, he drew me aside to find out more about our preparations, the standard of the unit and the nature of our assignment. He wanted –

to use one of his own idiosyncratic expressions – to be sure that we 'had the cleaning kit under control'.

As always, the general was direct in his questions and precise in his opinions. I appreciated that. It meant I knew what I was dealing with.

When our conversation turned to the senior officers, Knud Bartels asked whether I was comfortable with the people on the team, and whether there was anybody I was keeping a particular eye on. At first I was very diplomatic. I wanted to give the impression that I knew all the officers, including their strengths and weaknesses, and it seemed to work. I sensed that my account was being taken in the right spirit, and didn't expect any further questions.

I was mistaken. The general went right for the jugular, asking concrete questions about the specific officer I knew might give us trouble. He mentioned three or four issues he had managed to sniff out, and wanted to know what I thought about them.

I explained that I was aware of these issues, and described how I was planning to deal with the problems they might entail. The general let me say my piece, so that I could get everything off my chest. When I had finally finished my report – that's how it must have sounded – he looked me straight in the eye and said:

'If you're in doubt, you're not in doubt!'

He concluded by saying he could tell that I *wasn't* in any doubt about my decision, so that was that. I clearly had the cleaning kit under control, so he wished me a good trip to Kosovo.

I thanked him, but inside I was cursing. I knew deep down that I didn't have as much control over the cleaning kit as I had made out.

'If you're in doubt, you're not in doubt' was a phrase that ended up haunting me in Kosovo. I thought about that bloody sentence every time I had problems with the officer in question – and problems I certainly had. It was almost uncanny how much energy I expended on him, dealing with friction within the team and his colleagues' frustration.

> 'If you're in doubt, you're not in doubt.'

As a leader, I had to be inclusive and open, acting as if I had time for everybody and was above petty disputes, but the truth is, I was absolutely infuriated that despite several warnings I had kept him on the team.

The phrase also proved highly significant for me a few years later, when I was preparing for the mission in Afghanistan. I promised myself that I wouldn't end up in the same situation again. If I was in doubt about anybody in the organisation, I would remember the general's words.

Was it necessary? Yes, it certainly was. I had to make several tough decisions about privates, sergeants and officers who, ultimately, didn't come with us to Afghanistan. There were many reasons. Some were talented, but too young. Some weren't physically up to it. Some had difficulty finding their place in the unit because the chemistry simply wasn't right.

When I found myself in a dilemma, able to see both pros and cons to keeping a certain person on the team, I usually let the general's words decide: if I was in doubt, then I wasn't really in doubt. The mission awaiting us in Afghanistan would demand the most out of everybody in the unit. Our focus would have to be on accomplishing the mission, meaning we'd be concentrating on military issues and nothing else. There was no room for power struggles, dissatisfaction, long faces or an 'I know best' attitude. The military operations that had to be carried out in Afghanistan would be bloody, frightening and potentially traumatic. In that kind of situation there is simply no room for internal squabbles.

It's incredible how a single sentence can have enormous impact on your approach to leadership. I know that other leaders have also taken it to heart and use it actively. I consider it an important part of the next phase, which takes place after you have worked out a strategy and identified what training and development is needed to carry it out.

The next step is to put together a group of people who can execute the strategy and undergo the appropriate training. It's time to assemble a dream team!

During this phase it's important to challenge yourself. I know that most leaders have been in a situation where, like me, they weren't sure how to fill a particular position. Should it be this person or that one? Should it be an internal candidate or someone from outside? When you're in the latter situation, my advice would be to ask yourself whether the person you have in mind is really only in the running because he or she already works in your organisation.

To put it bluntly: are you trying to make the organisation fit the strategy or the other way around?

You can choose to lie to yourself, of course, tinkering a little with the strategy and the training so that the internal candidate fits the post. That was what I did in Kosovo.

But if you keep adjusting the strategy to suit your employees, you'll probably end up somewhere you don't want to be. The results will speak for themselves – and it won't be good news.

You can also choose to trust the strategy and insist on the training needed to live up to it. If you're still in doubt about whether a particular employee fits in, then you're not really in doubt. You're not going to change the strategy or the training. You're going to find another person for the role. That was what I did in Afghanistan.

This isn't a magic bullet. I know that finding the right employees is complicated and multifaceted – you could write a whole book just about that. But for me, it boils down to these three words: trust, hope and honesty.

Trust the strategy.

Hope that the training is doing its job.

Be honest when it comes to choosing employees – from top to bottom, from the director right down to the people in the engine room.

These three concepts are closely interlinked, and together they are all essential to obtaining outstanding results. You know where your own weak spots are, just as I know where mine are. I have often seen companies or military units institute a great plan or strategy, put all the right training in place and do a good job of supporting the strategy, but then stumble when it comes to honesty.

The most common mistake is to lose focus on finding the right people – both initially and during the process of adjusting the strategy. Typically, fine-tuning doesn't lead to changes among the staff: no new employees are recruited, no roles are replaced and none of the necessary training or professional development is carried out. That sort of thing is often neglected.

As a leader, you have to ask yourself on a regular basis: how often does my company make changes? Where are our priorities as we put the team together? How honest are we being, how faithful to the strategy?

To put it bluntly: are you trying to make the organisation fit the strategy or the other way around?

You have to be true to yourself and to the task ahead of you. If you realise that the team around you sadly isn't the team you need to win the war, or to bring your company or local authority outstanding results, then you have to deal with the consequences.

In my eyes, the strategy always has to be the guiding principle in the way you organise the company, although obviously it's also not a good idea to overhaul your entire staff once a year. Strategic planning means you need to take the long view: I'm talking about a multi-year, long-term perspective. Everything else is just action plans that support the strategy in the present.

Keeping a constant focus on whether you have the right team behind you is essential, so you must be willing to make changes on an ongoing basis. This holds true throughout the organisation. A board of directors should focus on replacing top managers when the situation demands it. There needs to be a plan in place that sets out when the change will happen, who could be a potential successor and what skills he or she needs to have in light of the overall strategy.

There is, for instance, a world of difference between a company during a consolidation phase and one engaged in a wildly creative and innovative process of development.

Keeping a constant focus on whether you have the right team behind you is essential, so you must be willing to make changes on an ongoing basis.

Wouldn't they demand a different kind of senior manager? I think so. Could the consequences prove challenging? I think so too.

You assemble a team for the game you're about to play. That's how it works in the football-ing world. Here, substitutions are par for the course; they happen every week. It doesn't have to be that common in industry or local government, but the board of directors, senior management and individual bosses have to have this consideration firmly in mind: have I put together the right team – today, tomorrow and for the future?

For me personally, and for my unit, it was an enormous asset to be able to leave for Afghanistan secure in the knowledge that the most important key people had been identified and placed in the organisation. Having seized the opportunity to assemble your dream team, as a leader you then have a solid foundation from which to accomplish your goals.

As previously mentioned, the strongest leaders I know have been found in the field, during exercises and in times of war. Only when people are under serious pressure, tired and hungry, does it become clear who has the professionalism, composure, perspective and ability to be caring towards their colleagues.

I have often said to bosses in both the private and public sectors that they should be grateful for the financial crisis. I mentioned this earlier in the book, but I want to emphasise it again, because so many managers seem to forget it. If they were observant, they would have noticed who among their staff could perform in a crisis, who managed to keep things together, who earned respect, and who was able to take charge when the pressure was at its most intense. Those are precisely the leaders who should be identified and developed – the ones worth betting on.

Before the Afghanistan mission I travelled to Iraq, where Danish soldiers were involved in fierce fighting, to talk to the commanders on the ground about precisely this issue. I wanted them to help me find the soldiers and leaders who had proved themselves to be talented, robust and caring.

During a patrol, I accompanied a young sergeant who had been recommended to me. I immediately sensed that he had a fantastically professional group around him. He was highly professionally and competent, and there was something about him that made you feel he would always be ready to lead from the front, listen to his soldiers and – after careful consideration – follow some of their advice. I discovered, too, that in pressured situations he always found the energy to be caring, both towards his own soldiers and the local Iraqis. I felt not a moment's doubt. I wanted him with me in Afghanistan – and I wanted him on the front lines.

You have to decide for yourself whether it's the financial crisis, military exercises or something altogether different that will help you to find the right leaders and employees for your dream team. Whatever it is, my message is relatively simple: theoretical training can be an excellent supplement and give you plenty of leadership inspiration, but not even a degree from the best business or management school in the world will guarantee you a perfect leader. Leadership is, and has always been, practical work.

It's funny – though you see it all over the place – that leaders are selected almost automatically on the strength of their professional qualifications. Let me give you a typical example from a hospital: a senior doctor has climbed the ranks and practises a style of leadership that is anything but first-class. He is fiercely talented within his area of expertise, but he's had no training in practical leadership; he lacks the capacity for it, and in many cases the interest, too.

The same can be said of engineers, IT experts, lawyers and many other professions. We can all think of examples of people who are experts in a particular field, then are suddenly thrust into a leadership position and, unfortunately, turn out to be completely unsuited to it.

Leadership positions bring money and prestige – they will always be coveted. That's not going to change. But it's worth thinking about why so many people evidently imagine that unique *professional* expertise is synonymous with unique *leadership* expertise.

If at all possible, I would encourage you to switch off autopilot when it's time to choose a leader within a particular professional area. It's important to challenge potential leaders to consider whether it's primarily leadership they're after or whether, in reality, they want professional skills.

Are there alternative solutions to just automatically making a professionally competent lawyer, doctor, engineer or chemist a leader? And if it absolutely has to be the best engineer, what challenges are involved – for both the engineer and the company as a whole? Being a leader isn't a side-line. It's a full-time job. Would it mean that you're about to lose your best engineering brain? Perhaps!

We have to recognise that when we put a specialist in a leadership role, we're going to lose something of the specialist, all other things being equal. And we've got a leader with a number of weak spots – that's almost unavoidable. But it's not a catastrophe. It just means the leader is like the rest of us. However, it becomes a problem if this isn't addressed, or dealt with, and can develop into a catastrophe.

The same is true of generalists. People with a BA in everything –

> **We have to recognise that when we put a specialist in a leadership role, we're going to lose something of the specialist.**

and therefore sometimes nothing – can be a challenge for any organisation. The important thing is to uncover and get rid of their flaws, or at least bring them to light. It's hiding them that's catastrophic. Sooner or later, they'll always surface.

'Knowing your own weaknesses is a strength.' This line can sound a bit New Age-y and therapy-ish. But, ultimately, it's imperative as a leader to be aware of the kernel of truth within it: the sooner you realise there's something you're just not that good at, the sooner you can take this into consideration when you put together your team.

Speaking for myself, I'm almost frighteningly bad with numbers. I'm ok when it comes to my household budget – I make sure there's a reasonable balance between income and expenditure – and I've got a handle on the budgets and accounts of the units, companies and organisations for which I've been financially responsible, but that's where my competence ends.

That is why I have always taken care to surround myself with talented number-crunchers, letting them know they have a weighty responsibility on their shoulders. They are deliberately chosen for their pedagogical ability as well as their numerical gifts, so that they can translate complicated number-talk into a language I can understand.

Once you've acknowledged that you come up short in some departments, you shouldn't be afraid to let others know. In my experience, it only engenders respect when a senior manager is willing to discuss areas where they're less strong. For example, if employees can also see that the finance director on the board compensates for his/her deficiencies to a great extent, it sends a strong signal. And if, on top of that, the managing director can pepper their acknowledgement with a pinch of humour and self-irony, the response will be twice as positive still.

This is genuine, trustworthy leadership. Fake leaders who try to give the impression that they can do everything are generally perceived as untrustworthy. In the long run, they can't keep it up. More on that later.

Let me sum this up with a question: if you have a clear strategy, a training programme designed to support it, and a team with the right leaders and employees to carry it out, will everything go smoothly?

The immediate answer is yes, but I do want to underscore two issues that are also important when putting together a dream team, and which you have to bear in mind before you launch into the challenges ahead.

The first is about power versus dynamism in a leadership context. The second is about the external organisation you establish around you.

First, a little on the difference between leadership power and leadership dynamism. When you put together your dream team, it is crucial to focus on these two concepts. Does that sound cryptic? There's an explanation coming up.

By power, I mean the right and duty you have as a leader to hire and fire people. Your authority to make decisions about salaries and reprimands, to give instructions and lay down rules – fundamentally, to do what you feel is the right thing, right then. That power has to be clearly defined.

By dynamism, I'm referring to a quality of your personal leadership. Dynamism means you can step up and take charge, motivating, encouraging and inspiring your employees to excel.

Results aren't achieved through exercising power alone, but in combination with dynamism.

If the scope of your power as a leader isn't clearly defined, it creates uncertainty, and you will find that your dynamism is drained and you become vague. If you are constantly unsure of the extent of your power, it will saturate everything you do, and in the worst-case scenario it could lead to your employees perceiving you as weak and untrustworthy, 'because he never gets anything done'.

Results aren't achieved through exercising power alone, but in combination with dynamism.

When I was a commander on international missions, in general, I found that there was a clear link between my power and my dynamism as a leader. I wielded enormous power. If I wanted something to happen, in the vast majority of cases it ended up happening. I didn't have to accommodate anybody else; I had the opportunity to act like the leader I personally wanted to be.

Previously, I had experienced exactly the opposite situation at an office at Defence Command. There, I had essentially no power as a leader. All my decisions had to be approved three, four, even five levels above me. Every time I had to convey dynamism, the people I was talking to knew perfectly well that everything I said would most likely be changed over the course of a few hours or days.

Regulations and guidelines meant that I frequently felt like an administrator, whose job was simply to carry out the rules, plans and checks that came down from above. I just had to 'fill in the blanks' as efficiently as possible, and that naturally affected my style of leadership.

It's a distinction that can be difficult to handle, and which challenges many of the leaders I have met, including those outside the military world. Many people find that their power is limited to the point where it hampers good, effective leadership. Leaders aren't given permission to be leaders.

I am always in favour of responsibilities and duties being clearly vested in the individual leaders who are interacting directly with others, so that they can bring all their dynamism to bear wherever its effect is greatest.

If you feel like a leader and you want to be one, but you are only being used as an administrator, then something is wrong. You have to speak up. If all you're doing is running systems and processes, then that may be effective in the short-term – it might work for now – but it's absolutely not constructive for you or for the company in the long-term.

There's nothing wrong with administrators. We need them. But we shouldn't force our best leaders into administrative jobs. When you're putting together your dream team, it's vitally important to put the right people in the right roles and, among other things, that involves finding leaders who can lead and administrators who can administrate. Don't let these terms get watered down.

What role do you feel you currently have: are you a leader or an administrator? I think deep down you know the answer. It's an issue near and dear to virtually all the leaders I know. Many of them complain about finding themselves in a situation where everything has to be expressed in terms of what's measurable or quantifiable, even though everybody agrees that's not always possible. Does that sound familiar? Can you do anything about it?

'Spreadsheet' leadership can – best-case scenario – be useful for brief, intense periods, when things reach crunch time. But in the long-term, companies and organisations survive on passionate leadership and the ability to encourage engagement, creativity and camaraderie, and those things can't be directly measured.

Finding a balance between the role of leaders and that of administrators is an incredibly important discipline for senior managers, but if they can't carry it off then they run a serious risk of losing cohesion within the organisation. You see it unfold very quickly. Employees lose confidence in the management, eroding their credibility. If the people on the ground sense that those at the top are only interested in columns, graphs and the bottom line, then things pretty soon take a turn for the worse. And they can go just as wrong if employees in the field don't understand the framework within which the company now operates.

My point is that we need to respect both leaders and administrators. Lately, it seems to me that the latter have come to be valued more highly. 'If it can be measured, it should be measured' is a philosophy on the advance, and recently there has been a marked focus on terms like *controlling* and *key performance indicators (KPI)*.

For me, this sets alarm bells ringing: if it goes too far, it can prove damaging for any company. Leaders who begin developing into conformist administrators lose focus on their own leadership. They get comfortable. Common sense goes out the window. If the company has also indicated that people who concentrate on target figures, tables and KPIs are the ones who get to build a career there, then it's in serious trouble. It will end up lacking real leaders – the ones who can show passionate, credible and innovative leadership.

This is why, as a leader, I would advise against treating administrators and specialists as if they have all the answers. You're the one in charge. The experts in your organisation are there solely to support you as you make decisions – not to steer, but to support. Their input is what underpins the strategy. You should, of course, take advice from lawyers, economists, logistics specialists and HR bosses seriously, but it's your responsibility to see it simply as individual pieces of input. You should be concerned with the big picture, and as a leader you should teach your experts to understand it too, and their supporting roles within it.

Leadership is about intuition, ethics, responsibility, decency and consideration, which is why leadership is a discipline in its own right. You have to be able to balance hardcore information from lawyers and economists with your own sense of what's happening on the ground, supported by HR, union representatives and feedback from customers or clients. And obviously you too should have a high level of professional expertise – this goes without

Leadership is about intuition, ethics, responsibility, decency and consideration, which is why leadership is a discipline in its own right.

saying, but it's important to remember.

Understanding the various worlds within your company is crucial to success as a leader. Being aware of everyone's roles requires a genuine interest in what's going on, both in the engine room and on the bridge. It's your task to create a framework that takes everybody into account.

If you succeed, you will be able to develop a company where everybody respects everybody else's work. You will also create an appreciation for the fact that some people work in a potentially chaotic environment, so they may not always be able to fill out their reports on time and with 100% accuracy. Show understanding and respect for that when you're in the administrative office.

It works the other way around, too: when you're on the front line, try to accept that everybody in the background is doing their best to support you. This mutual appreciation is what characterises a dream team. Try to create an appreciation for the different working conditions across the company. That is how you maintain a sense of cohesion.

After the Afghanistan mission, I witnessed an unforgettable example of an administrator lacking understanding for the units deployed on the ground. As part of the evaluation of what we had achieved, I had a discussion with a senior civil servant who – quite genuinely – thought we had used too much ammunition when fighting the Taliban. His numbers showed that we had gone through much more ammunition than they had anticipated back in Copenhagen. So he had wondered – and this is what he wanted to discuss with me – whether they could introduce a per-soldier quota, so that they would learn not to waste ammunition. It would be a good idea, he thought, to give each soldier a certain number of cartridges then, once they had been used up, any further ammunition would come out of the soldier's pay.

At first I thought this was a joke. But when I saw his unamused expression, I became seriously worried. This was an example of two worlds not understanding each other. His intention was noble enough: as a soldier you should think carefully before using ammunition. He was also right to point out that we had used more ammunition than expected in Afghanistan, which was a problem from a financial perspective.

But what he didn't understand, even after I did my best to explain, was that soldiers already tried desperately hard not to waste any ammunition. When you're deployed in the Green Zone in Helmand, far from your base, you only have the ammunition you can carry with you. And the worst thing that could possibly happen is to run out of ammunition. If you're standing in a field of maize, in the middle of a direct confrontation with the Taliban, without any more cartridges – every soldier knows what that means. In all likelihood, certain death.

Had our soldiers been on the verge of that situation? Yes, many times. Nobody forgets that kind of experience.

The civil servant insisted that we had used too much ammunition, so he thought that his suggestion should at least come into effect during exercises at home in Denmark. I disagreed with that too. A soldier deployed on the front lines shouldn't be thinking about the financial consequences of using ammunition. He's already automatically focusing on using the fewest possible number of cartridges during combat. The worst thing that could happen to him isn't being sent a bill for the cartridges. It's much more dangerous than that.

This was an unpleasant reminder of the lack of understanding people can show for soldiers' operative conditions during wartime. It also taught me a lesson: as commanding officers, we must never forget that it is our responsibility to tell the bureaucrats sitting thousands of miles behind the front lines what the assignment actually entails on the ground.

With the dream team in place and the different types of officer put in posts that suited them, I felt that after six months' preparation we were ready for the Afghanistan mission. That proved not to be completely true. Over a series of conversations with previous commanders of similar missions in the Balkans, Iraq and Afghanistan – conversations that would have a decisive influence on my actions, and for which I'm deeply grateful today – the same issue kept cropping up: in their experience, the most demanding team was not the one with them on the mission. It was the one back home.

My colleagues talked about challenges they'd experienced with very senior military bosses, civil servants, the press and military courts, with political announcements from one end or another of the Danish parliament, and even with close colleagues who held various posts in ministries or at Defence Command.

Their advice was very clear: you need to protect yourself against pressure from back home. Many people will be on your side while the going's good. But if things suddenly start going badly, you'll find people are suddenly queuing up to wash their hands of you.

This wasn't particularly pleasant listening, but their advice was so clear and unambiguous that I had to take them very seriously. After all, every day in Helmand there would be a risk that something could go really wrong. As a commander, you always feel that it's up to you to take ultimate and extreme decisions. If the worst should happen and you make a fatal mistake, you can be sure that you'll hear about it from the people back home.

With help and support from friends and acquaintances, I made connections with a lawyer, three journalists and eight 'guardian angels' before I left for Afghanistan. I've had mentors in the civilian world for many years, and naturally they were also part of my network.

Many people will be on your side while the going's good. But if things suddenly start going badly, you'll find people are suddenly queuing up to wash their hands of you.

The lawyer kept a constant eye out for any sudden developments that would require him to begin work on my behalf. The three journalists helped by analysing the situation in the Danish media, giving me valuable

113

information about the potential dangers lurking around the corner. I weighed up possible scenarios with them, so I had a sense of what I might say if something bad happened.

Guardian angels – what are they? Being several thousand miles away from Denmark, I wouldn't be able to convey the nuances of what was happening in Afghanistan. I myself had witnessed how an organisation could go into meltdown off the back of unfounded rumours, biases and misunderstandings. So I needed good friends to keep things calm behind the scenes if people got the wrong end of the stick. I lined up close friends at the Foreign Office, the Ministry of Defence, Defence Command, the Army Operational Command and at the Royal Danish Military Academy. When something happened to us in Afghanistan, they would be there – both internally and in public – to emphasise that there was probably a good explanation, or at least two sides to the story.

During the mission I was forwarded many emails from former pupils at the military academy who were now in roles close to the top. They didn't always make for comforting reading. I could see how certain bosses at home in Denmark were enormously keen to pre-emptively cover themselves. Obviously, they didn't let me know that – officially I had plenty of support. But in emails circulating on the home front, their signals were very different – they used phrases like '… even if things go well and they get good results, we can't rule out …' and so on – and they gave all sorts of cautions and caveats about what might go wrong. They were trying to safeguard themselves and protect their own careers.

Perhaps I was too sensitive and naïve – I probably was – but it was a huge disappointment. My second-in-command, Mads Rahbek, was ice cold when it came to that sort of thing. His advice was that I shouldn't let myself be affected by weak bosses who were only along for the ride on the uptick, but weren't willing to face the downturn. As Mads said: 'Remember, Kim, loyalty is mainly a top-down thing, not the other way around. If you focus on that, nothing will go wrong.'

He was right. If all bosses followed that principle, staff would find that there was support from the top, right the way down. Wouldn't that create a strong sense of loyalty and cohesion?

I should emphasise that I had a great deal of support from the Minister of Defence, the Chief of Defence and the head of the Army Operational Command. I never got bcc'd on negative emails from them. The knowledge that I had support at the very highest level of command was incredibly significant for my daily activities in Afghanistan.

I and my second-in-command relied heavily on two colleagues in particular throughout the duration of our presence in Afghanistan: Colonel Lars R. Møller and Colonel Eigil Schjønning. I would be willing to follow those two through fire and water myself, and their support was invaluable.

The mission in Afghanistan had many facets that had nothing to do with leading soldiers into battle. I was in command of the large area around the commercial town of Gereshk, and had to think about setting up civil administration, schools and a healthcare system at the same time that as I was dealing with political attention, the critical eye of the press, relationships with other countries in the area and much more. The danger was that I would lose focus on the war itself and its conditions.

The Taliban were deeply embedded in the area when we arrived, and in order to have any chance of civil development we would have to get rid of them first. If I siphoned too many resources away from the core objective, which unfortunately was the military operations, we would be unable to set in motion the more positive and interesting developments for the local population.

The two colonels helped Mads and myself stay focused. It was useful to have the occasional friendly and well-intentioned dressing-down from respected colleagues. They reminded us that 'there is a time for war and a time for everything else afterwards – quickly, if possible, but afterwards'.

If you lose concentration when war is necessary, then you'll lose far too many soldiers. And you won't achieve your objectives.

If you lose concentration when war is necessary, then you'll lose far too many soldiers. And you won't achieve your objectives.

When, after the mission in Afghanistan, I gave an account of my experiences at internal briefings, I spoke openly about how I had protected myself through my relationships with a lawyer as well as journalists and 'guardian angels'. This didn't always go down very well.

It might, as one participant put it, give the impression that I didn't have much confidence in the system.

In a way, this was true. But when I think about all those emails I was sent during the mission, with their hedging and caveats, I'm in no doubt that it was appropriate. And during the mission it was very reassuring to know that I had a solid network behind me.

I would encourage you to think along the same lines as a leader: it can be incredibly rewarding to have advisors outside of the organisation you work for.

As a young manager, you shouldn't be afraid to turn to older and more experienced leaders for support. In my experience, they are more than happy to pass on their experience, and are willing to listen and help you. Develop a connection with them. My mentors have all been older than me – they have had various backgrounds, and I have maintained the relationships – including in my later job at the embassy in Paris and at the royal court.

Mentors can be vital, especially during tough times. They inspire you, giving you an extra impetus and offering a critical yet constructive perspective. They look at things in more nuanced way than you do, because you're 100% engaged in your task and, therefore, tend towards tunnel vision. It's great to have friends who have a bird's-eye view, and can give you the essential nuances and alternative angles.

Putting together a dream team is therefore also about identifying a support network outside your company.

I would like to end this chapter by describing a personal experience of the more unfortunate variety. If you yourself are a senior manager, I hope you can use this as a salutary tale.

Not long after coming home, I was supposed to appear at an event that also included a prominent politician. I was sitting – wearing my uniform – backstage when the politician came in, nodded briefly and sat down in a chair directly facing me.

At that point we were engaged in heavy combat in Afghanistan and had lost many soldiers, but although we were waiting backstage for nearly twenty minutes, the politician wasn't moved to say a single word to me. Not one!

Usually, he never missed an opportunity to appear on television talking about our soldiers' important work in Afghanistan, about his support and – not least – his concern for them. But now he didn't utter a word.

As someone else in the room noted afterwards, 'He could at least have briefly mentioned something about his respect for the work you've all done out there, or expressed his sorrow and regret over the losses you've suffered. He could certainly have said something or other ...'.

It would have cost nothing to make some comment to me along those lines and, by extension, to the soldiers. I would have made sure to pass it on. But now I was taking something else away from our meeting.

Let this example be a reminder that, as a leader, you should always be aware of the signals you're sending out. It takes such a tiny amount of effort to show an interest in your employees – and it means so very much.

Don't forget that! Don't forget *them*!

In the previous chapters I have tried to lay out a framework for creating true excellence in leadership. It is absolutely vital to put time and energy into designing a unique strategy, into training like you fight, and into identifying the team best suited to the task. That framework is now in place.

The following chapters focus on the things that, in my experience, offer the best possible support for this framework. The next chapter is dedicated to stories about camaraderie within companies. I have touched on this already, but now I want to dig a little deeper.

CHAPTER 5

Establish Cohesion

IN 1997 I moved with my family onto a cobbled street behind the walls of Kastellet, a fortress in Copenhagen. Before long I started to notice something surprising: every morning a crowd of well-dressed young people, both men and women, came walking through Kastellet from Østerport Station, self-assured, purposeful and with a smile on their faces. It was obvious they were on their way to do something they were proud of and looking forward to.

'Just look how energetic they are, Tine,' I said. 'And they say the youth of today isn't what it used to be. Doesn't seem like we have much to worry about on that score!'

Who were these young people? I found out one morning when I happened to be going the same way. When we reached the esplanade, they disappeared into the head office of A.P. Moeller–Maersk. It turned out that most of them were shipping trainees.

Once I realised that, the passion they radiated should have come as no surprise – and it didn't. I was aware of the aura surrounding Maersk, and especially the shipping magnate Mærsk Mc-Kinney Møller. People were simply proud to be part of the company.

At that point I was teaching at the Royal Danish Military Academy, where I saw the same mixture of pride, self-confidence and passion among the dedicated young officers who were my students.

'You'll be judged by the little things,' I told my students, 'and if you do them with decency, you won't go far wrong.'

I'll return to the little things later in the chapter, but this is what I mean by doing things decently:

Some time later, during a run along the harbour, I had an experience that gave me pause for thought: in front of Maersk's head office stood a young couple taking a picture. At the same moment a sleek, chauffeur-driven silvery-grey BMW drew up, and out stepped Mærsk Mc-Kinney Møller. He was friendly towards the young couple, asking them where they came from (they turned out to be Australian tourists), and wanted to know if they liked the architecture. This led to a brief but very pleasant conversation that I followed avidly, and which resulted in him asking whether they would like to have their photograph taken with him, because he was the one responsible for the firm. Smiling ear to ear, he stood next to the surprised young couple, asked his driver to take the picture, then wished them a pleasant stay in Copenhagen.

He didn't take the time to talk to them for the benefit of the media or the public. I was the only other person around. It seemed that he simply couldn't resist getting out of the car to chat when he saw the young Australians. That, for me, is the very definition of doing things decently.

I see a direct connection between my impression of the young people on their way to work and Mærsk Mc-Kinney's treatment of the young Australians, and I find his example inspirational. When classic virtues like decency and honesty are deeply ingrained in a company – from the most senior executive to the newest employee – you can create an extraordinarily powerful team. When everybody feels a sense of passion and pride, you'll be surprised at the stamina and cohesion it produces – and what results you can achieve.

As a leader, you have to be focused on creating the kind of camaraderie that makes everybody pull together.

You can't raise your game 100%, but if you can push ten employees to do at least 10% better, it has an impact on the bottom line. If the opposite happens – if you destroy the sense of camaraderie and cohesion, and your employees lose their passion and stop taking pleasure in their work – there is no doubt that your company will be in trouble.

When classic virtues like decency and honesty are deeply ingrained in a company – from the most senior executive to the newest employee – you can create an extraordinarily powerful team.

Once you've experienced war and seen soldiers on the brink of exhaustion, having lost on average ten kilos in weight and many comrades, you realise how much potential there is in terms like cohesion, camaraderie and passion.

What made soldiers keep heading out through the gate to patrol in the Green Zone, despite the danger to their lives? In the evaluations after they returned home, it was interesting to hear their answers.

'We didn't want to let anybody down,' was the most common response. The soldiers didn't want to let down their comrades, their unit, their regiment or their country, and they didn't want to let themselves down either. They didn't want anybody to be able to turn around afterwards and say that they hadn't done their best. A strong sense of cohesion means that every single employee has that embedded in their DNA.

When you're newly employed at a company, you probably don't want to be immediately confronted with the

As a leader, you have to be focused on creating the kind of camaraderie that makes everybody pull together.

question, 'Do you promise not to let anybody down?' In any case, this would be a silly question to ask on day one. It's a feeling that has to be built up gradually, as you come to identify with the company's values. Eventually, you find you can represent the product, that your colleagues are there for you when you need them, and that you have confidence in the management.

In my case, being an officer in the Royal Lifeguards has had enormous personal significance. We're a little odd in many ways, I must admit, but we have deep roots in a history that stretches back more than 350 years. More than 2,000 soldiers from the Royal Lifeguards have lost their lives in battle, and our shared heritage means that as an officer you show respect for the missions, challenges, losses and suffering that our comrades have been through before us. That's why 'Once a guardsman, always a guardsman' is our motto.

My training at the Army Non-Commissioned Officer School in Sønderborg, where South Jutland's chequered history always feels very present, and at the Royal Danish Military Academy in Frederiksberg Palace in Copenhagen also had a profound influence on me. Wandering around those historic places shapes you as an officer. You don't realise it at the time, yet slowly but surely it creeps up on you, creating your identity. It affects the way you act – you discover that pretty quickly once your life is on the line, if not before.

Many people have tried to convince me that this history doesn't mean anything when it really counts, but I don't buy that, and it isn't borne out by my own experience. Assignments must always be carried out, dire though the consequences may be. We must always be ready to accept difficult challenges. This was constantly at the back of my mind when I was a commander in Afghanistan. It was also what tipped the scales whenever I was in a situation where I could have taken the easy way out, avoiding the tough stuff and palming off the most difficult tasks onto others, yet chose not to.

In Krajina I even heard myself utter the words, 'To the last man and the last cartridge'. It's an order you feel through your whole body when you give it, and which underscores how deadly serious the circumstances are.

When the Croatian offensive was in full flow, I realised that refugees might try to seek shelter in our main camp, so I asked two of my most trusted officers to prepare it to take them in. I told them I had decided that any refugees who turned up would be defended 'to the last man and the last cartridge'.

No refugees came to our camp. The approximately 10,000 Krajina Serbs who fled the area went to Bosnia-Herzegovina instead, but I will never forget the moment that, for the first time in my life, I uttered the words, 'to the last man and the last cartridge'.

You don't let anyone down!

Pride, professionalism, camaraderie, comradeship, passion, cohesion – all these terms are about emotion, and you can't put that in a spreadsheet. Staying focused on how important these things are is a major challenge as a leader. They have to be prioritised.

If you haven't personally experienced how valuable they can be, I have found that it can be difficult, unfortunately, to convince others of that value. They sound right, but really understanding them in depth – including from a financial perspective and in terms of resources – is difficult.

The issue is simply that if you pare away history, camaraderie and – with it – a sense of identity from your company, you'll turn your employees into passion-less robots, to put it bluntly. They might get the job done as management dictates, but they will do so without any real commitment or reflection. This is true not just in the military, but in general – in all public and private companies.

In the military it means a lot to hold a parade, or to have stars on your shoulder or a parachutist badge on your chest. Simply wearing the uniform has a big impact, which is why it would be disastrous if – just as an example – someone decided that officers no longer had to wear a uniform day-to-day.

Everything that can be done to encourage camaraderie, cohesion and values should have a leader's undivided attention. It matters where you fall in the annual 'image' rankings, and how you are seen by your employees and the world at large. I firmly believe that that will be an important parameter in a future where qualified employees may be lacking.

Everything that can be done to encourage camaraderie, cohesion and values should have a leader's undivided attention.

Many companies are thinking more and more about how to develop the kind of storytelling that will attract the best employees and keep the most talented ones. But it's not enough to tell stories about the company being notoriously creative, giving you free rein, having a high level of professionalism or offering development schemes to its employees. It's just as important to be completely clear about the company's core values, what it stands for and the kind of signals it wants to give out.

You could just call it prestige. Employees want to work somewhere they can relate to. If they have strong feelings about the company and what it stands for, they won't want to let it down.

Maintaining a strong spirit of camaraderie therefore requires a lot of input from management, but it mustn't come at the cost of losing focus on small, everyday chores and challenges – and this brings us back to my point about being mindful of 'the little things'.

It took several years before I understood that utterly mundane things can have a big impact on employees' day-to-day lives, and are crucial to ensuring their support and respect for you as a leader.

You should take their working conditions seriously. What may seem to you like minor details – a dead light bulb, the overly long queue in the canteen – are actually quite significant, and it's all too easy to forget or neglect these things.

Often, it's the little things that your employees judge you by. If you don't deal with these small, irritating issues, they'll lose faith in you. You *have* to do something about the things they think aren't working. You can wait until tomorrow to get them onside with the grand, overarching strategy. For now, just change the damn light bulb!

You'd be surprised how big an impact it can have to listen actively and react to things that aren't working on the ground. Focus on them – resolve the problem quickly and properly. If you do, your employees will probably still be onside when they're facing bigger problems than a broken light bulb.

You'll only find out about these small, irritating issues by walking around the corridors, a mug of coffee in your hand, listening to your employees and talking to them. Then they'll probably get you involved, and maybe even come up with suggestions that turn out to be brilliant. The best ideas often come from employees thinking along new and different lines. They rarely originate with the board of directors.

Walking among your employees, being visible, listening and actively communicating naturally leads to another area you should prioritise as a leader: communication. This has sometimes given me trouble over the years. I don't mind admitting that I have been taken aback by how much emphasis is needed on communicating promptly and purposefully.

Employees who lack information – and therefore don't understand the point of what they're doing – can't perform well or take initiative, so the sense of cohesion you've built up won't translate into concrete results. Or, to put it the other way round, if the prompt and purposeful information gets through to everybody, you will find that your employees can't resist getting involved. A natural and curious leader will discover that little nuggets of gold start to appear almost of their own accord. I am absolutely convinced that the upsurge of innovative, imaginative and creative companies in industry is fed by the vast number

Employees who lack information – and therefore don't understand the point of what they're doing – can't perform well or take initiative.

of suggestions coming from employees. Making everybody part of the team is an enormous asset.

If you feel that communication is your strong suit, then feel free to take a little test – from me to you: how often, as a leader, are you confronted with the following comment from your employees: 'Hold on, you're giving us too much information!'

Not very often, I would imagine.

When I took on my first leadership role, I thought I was keeping everyone fully apprised of everything. So it came as a surprise to find that my soldiers needed more information.

'But I tell them almost everything I hear about our assignments,' I thought. But that was not how they saw it.

Did I wise up over the years? Would my employees say that I've got better at communicating? I hope so, but I have to admit that it's difficult to answer with a resounding yes. The need for information seems to be inexhaustible and ever-present. It's an area that requires constant attention.

So what have I learnt about authentic communication?

First and foremost, I have learnt that messages should be conveyed in a way that makes sense. If you use specialised jargon – if you're a technologically orientated company, for instance – then that technical language can be a communication-killer. But intra-company communication also requires translation: people must be able to understand and apply what you're saying at all levels. You can't expect the cohesion you've built up to create results if your employees don't understand what the management is trying to convey.

If you need to communicate something of a financial or legal nature, it's no use presenting the news in legalese or using convoluted turns of phrase. Employees may interpret what you're saying in vastly different ways, even if you think it's crystal clear.

> **Employees may interpret what you're saying in vastly different ways, even if you think it's crystal clear.**

Once I realised that communication was a perpetual challenge, I tried to tackle things another way. I often asked for feedback from people at various levels of the organisation, to hear what they thought about what we as senior leaders had written before sending those messages out unit-wide.

Often, employees had this response: 'Fine, but what does this mean for me?' This is a good and relevant question. It often helped us to formulate the memos so that they were easier for employees to understand, with an increased focus on describing in concrete terms what they actually meant on an individual level.

It's one thing to write clearly. Whether your employees believe what you're trying to tell them is another. Authentic communication should ideally reflect a situation that the employees recognise: if they feel that what's being communicated doesn't actually correspond to reality, they will be surprised and start to disengage, sapping the overall sense of cohesion.

Not even the most effusive description of the company's general health can change the fact that, if all its employees are convinced that there are job cuts in the offing, then there probably are. The management will be aware of it too. So stop dressing it up as good news or giving a false impression of the situation. Some people might be tempted to believe that it's better to prettify what you're saying, but that hasn't been my experience. Employees have the right to expect prompt answers when faced with uncertainty, whether about budget cuts, job losses, new and exciting tasks in the pipeline, or a takeover by a capital investment company. Just tell it like it is!

One of our most important assets as Danes is a healthy scepticism towards authority. Our hierarchies tend to be fairly shallow, and we can easily make our opinions known to the management. I'm convinced that this is a key part of why Denmark has so often been cited in studies as one of the world's most innovative countries.

This anti-authoritarian streak in our culture means that as leaders we are more inclined to look kindly on critical questions from employees. If you encourage people to ask questions, if you act on them and you aren't afraid to admit that a previous decision was wrong or stupid, you're opening up an honest dialogue that will guide you to the best possible solutions.

I would go so far as to claim that people with anti-authoritarian tendencies can actually make the most loyal employees. How does that work? Well, if you show that you're not afraid of them speaking their mind – indeed, quite the contrary – and if you take the time to explain your own point of view, then they will always defend you and your actions. In all of my many different jobs, I've found that if you don't let your employees down, they won't let you down either.

A proactive and fiery management, and a group of employees who are just as curious and challenging, can be a wonderfully powerful combination.

Embrace the provocative, anti-authoritarian 'problem children', because they are the ones who will help you as a leader. They might seem like prima donnas, but it's prima donnas who will make your company move forward; you should be rolling out the red carpet instead of seeing them as irritating troublemakers. Deep down, they want the best for the company, so give them some space.

A team of employees who never ask questions will never come up with out-of-the-box suggestions or challenge the management, and that's a serious warning sign. If it's not simply down to fear, it will most likely be a sign of a lack of interest, engagement and passion.

It has also been my experience that it's better to discuss things face to face than to send round memos or emails. You need documents, of course, but as a leader nothing is more effective than your sheer presence. Grab a cup of coffee and head down the hallway: walk the talk. It's not a waste of time. It will benefit you as a leader, and you'll end up saving time.

Once you've got a strong sense of camaraderie in place, and the ability to communicate in a manner that's trustworthy and inspires confidence, you'll be well on your way to creating cohesion within your company. I just want to mention one further element that can be difficult, but also incredibly rewarding: the cultural diversity inherent to a workforce that includes people from many different countries collaborating within the same company or organisation.

A team of employees who never ask questions will never come up with out-of-the-box suggestions or challenge the management, and that's a serious warning sign.

'Don't ask me how I'm doing ever again!'

This was the blunt response I got from one of my Lithuanian soldiers. It was August 1995, and the Croatians had just finished their military offensive Operation Storm, so I was more or less constantly travelling around to our various outposts. For me, a natural part of my interest in the soldiers, Danish as well as Lithuanian, was to ask how they were doing. It felt completely appropriate to me.

But it didn't to him. He was a small, stocky guy of around thirty to thirty-five, very physically fit, with short blonde hair. He had been trained in the elite Soviet unit Spetsnaz, which is well known as one of the toughest special operations units in the world. He was used to a leadership style that centred around strict, rigid discipline, where soldiers didn't ask questions and – equally – officers didn't enquire how their people were doing. Quite simply, he didn't understand my question, and he was well and truly fed up with me regularly showing up and asking about his wellbeing.

I stood there speechless, completely at a loss. What had he just said to me?

He was saying quite clearly that he didn't want to hear any more about my pseudo-psychological interest in his mental state.

It came as a surprise to find that my interest could be interpreted in such a negative light, because I could see that lots of our soldiers weren't coping well with the harsh experiences of wartime. But it was also a learning experience for my thirty-year-old self, one that I was able to take away with me. The Lithuanian's remark lodged deep inside my brain: I didn't have a clear enough understanding of his background or the cultural differences that made him react as he did.

Just as I have worked constantly on communication as a key part of leadership, my attempts to understand and learn about – and from – other cultures have become increasingly important. I must acknowledge that as a leader I haven't always been quick enough on the uptake in that area, and I have also seen many of the companies I have worked with fail because they didn't seriously engage with other cultures. It requires a tremendous effort to boost cultural understanding.

1995 was the first time I was responsible for foreign soldiers – thirty-three Lithuanians, to be precise – as part of the peace-keeping mission around Krajina, now part of Croatia, which I have previously mentioned. Only three of the Lithuanians spoke English.

Prior to the journey, all my focus had been on understanding the opposing sides in the conflict, the Serbs and the Croatians. I read up on their history, attended lectures about Serbian and Croatian culture and studied living conditions in the Balkans. So before we left for Krajina, I felt reasonably well equipped to understand the culture I would encounter there.

But I knew virtually nothing about the culture in a Baltic country like Lithuania, which had only recently started to develop its own armed forces and was therefore building on the traditions of the Soviet army.

This was a mistake, and unfortunately it was a mistake I repeated some years later when I was given responsibility for French soldiers in Kosovo in 2005 and British, Czech and Afghan soldiers in Helmand Province in 2007. Before our deployment, I was focused on understanding the Taliban, the local warlords, the political climate in Denmark and the media coverage of the international mission in Afghanistan, but I didn't learn anything about the nationalities for which, as commander, I was responsible. In hindsight, I have to admit that I wasn't properly prepared for that part of my duties. I'm not saying that my leadership of them was catastrophically poor, but my knowledge of their mentalities and historical and cultural backgrounds wasn't really deep enough.

There is a big difference between the way we lead, speak, give orders, engage with people – I could go on. Even within Scandinavia, where culturally we perceive ourselves as much the same, differences pretty quickly emerge in terms of how we act, form relationships and find solutions.

Here, I just want to note that we have two ears and only one mouth. It's perhaps especially wise in a multicultural context to listen twice as much as we speak. If you actively listen, you will find that you need to use situation-specific leadership. Different nationalities demand different approaches to leadership. There are no one-size-fits-all solutions here.

Here, I just want to note that we have two ears and only one mouth. It's perhaps especially wise in a multicultural context to listen twice as much as we speak.

Instead, this is an invitation to understand ourselves better, whatever our nationality. It's always instructive – in fact, probably vitally necessary – to pay attention to the way other people perceive us. It teaches us to behave with more understanding and makes us more understandable to others.

Think back to your own company or organisation. To what extent have you and other leaders actively and deliberately – and I mean genuinely actively and deliberately – put resources towards understanding the Germans, Americans, Filipinos, Turks, Brazilians or Norwegians who work for you, or who you work closely with? To what extent has their presence affected your leadership style? What have you as a company learned from other nationalities? What influence have they had on your strategy and the training you carry out?

Personally, I learned an incredible amount about the significance of understanding other cultures when, from 2009 to 2012, I worked as a diplomat in Paris, with detours to Madrid and The Hague. Working alongside diplomats from many different countries was a powerful motivator to immerse myself in other nations' values, cultures and histories.

Let me give you an example. In Paris, my attitude with regards to when meetings should begin didn't get me very far: they should begin on time! That had always been my experience. Out of respect for your own time, but especially for that of others, you have a duty to begin punctually. After all, people have other commitments in their diaries too.

I found, however, that emphasising again and again that I preferred to start on time had little effect on the French. I put it in a friendly, humorous way, letting them know I understood that perhaps their lateness – often their excessive lateness – was due to traffic.

But that wasn't how the French saw it. It had nothing to do with traffic, or anything else for that matter. No, my esteemed French colleagues simply would not let their actions be dictated by a timetable with the same precision as I did. French people arrive as quickly as they can, neither earlier nor later, and they enter the room as if it were the most natural thing in the world, evidently not feeling in the least stressed about being late.

Perhaps it didn't stress out my French colleagues, but it stressed me out – at least initially. Eventually, I figured out that fighting it made no difference. I might as well try to adjust, although admittedly I found that rather difficult.

Fundamentally, I still felt that meetings should start on time. That's just how I am. But I learned to conduct my meetings in a slightly different way while I was stationed in Paris, and I had a thorough introduction to how other cultures think about agendas and meeting discipline.

In my current role at the royal court, one of my favourite duties is planning state visits. To do so we work in concert with the country we are either visiting or being visited by. Since 2012 I have been in close contact with China, Chile, Turkey, Slovakia, Croatia, Finland, the Netherlands, Vietnam and Indonesia – and by now I am well aware that I need to prepare extremely thoroughly before we collaborate on the planning process.

I am by no means an expert on cultural understanding, but after a good few years I have started deliberately and professionally working on it in a more systematic manner.

In the world of the military, camaraderie is all – or nearly all. You have to live and breathe for the unit of which you're a part.

It can take many years to build up a strong sense of camaraderie, but very little time to break it down. This can happen if the management neglects it, for instance, because it doesn't have an immediate impact on the bottom line. If that happens, before long the most talented employees will leave the company, because 'it's just like anywhere else'. I believe you need to stand out.

It can take many years to build up a strong sense of camaraderie, but very little time to break it down.

A strong sense of camaraderie is founded on passionate employees. Passion is etymologically related to the Latin word for suffering. It's often the case that – as in love – you have to suffer before you really experience it. Soldiers suffer together during wartime, but this also creates passion, because you look after each other and go on missions together even under the most trying circumstances, because it gives a meaning and a purpose to what you're doing. It has had that effect on me personally. I took great pride in being part of a more than 350-year history, where everybody knew that we were protecting something greater than ourselves, and what was asked of us was unambiguous: you never let anybody down.

I hope this chapter has challenged you to think about such notions as pride, cohesion and camaraderie. As I say, it requires deliberate managerial focus, but if you succeed your employees will be queuing up to join your team.

The next chapter will be no less challenging. It's about intuition.

As a leader, you must be willing to rely on your intuition, especially when it comes to the most difficult challenges. Are you able to rely on yours – even when it's time to make tough decisions?

CHAPTER 6

Trust Your Intuition

AT DAYBREAK ON 15 January 2008 I set in motion the last major military operation in Upper Gereshk Valley in Helmand Province.

In the icy rain and biting cold, several hundred Danish, British, Czech and Afghan soldiers moved north to flush out the final Taliban units in our area of responsibility. The weather was a formidable opponent. Fields and tracks had been turned into pools of mud, and it took several hours to cover a few kilometres. We received constant news that the Taliban were preparing to attack us with mortars, but thankfully that was a false alarm. Operation Thunder was a huge success. We achieved our objective without a single shot being fired.

It was the culmination of an offensive that had stretched out over six months and demanded a great deal of sacrifice from my soldiers, who had lost five of their comrades. Mixed in with our grief over this unbearable loss was a sense of relief and pride at having obtained the kind of results that, initially, we had hardly dared dream of. And now there were only a few weeks until we could hand over responsibility to another unit.

I spent several days at the forward operating bases Armadillo and Sandford, continuing to secure the area at close quarters. On 18 January I was called over to our command post at Sandford to read an official NATO document that had just been sent out to all allied headquarters.

When I saw the message blinking on the computer screen it was as if an electric shock ran through my whole body, from the roots of my hair down to my toes:

'Taliban has fled Upper Gereshk Valley.'

The note distilled the latest military intelligence, which said that the remaining commandants, along with an unknown number of fighters, had abandoned the Taliban's last two bastions in the valley, and that they had now sought refuge in a remote district in north-west Helmand – far away from my area of responsibility.

Furthermore, it announced that '... the Taliban currently judges the Upper Gereshk Valley to be much too dangerous for them. The commandants and fighters are afraid and demoralised. They fear further attacks from ISAF [the term for the international forces in Afghanistan – ed.] and have decided to flee to a more secure area where support for the Taliban is higher. The few Taliban members who have remained in the valley are chiefly locals with families. They have disarmed themselves by hiding their weapons or giving them to the fighters who have fled.'

When I re-read the document – I had to read it twice – I felt something akin to what Danish people must have experienced as they sat listening to the radio on the evening of 4 May 1945 and heard a voice say, 'This is London ...', followed by the news that the Germans had surrendered. It was, albeit on a smaller scale, a sense of freedom I could feel in my whole body. And I could see in the officers gathered around me that they were experiencing the same surge of emotion.

I already knew, of course, that we had succeeded in driving out the Taliban units, but receiving official confirmation still affected me deeply. Tiredness and relief washed over me, and tears ran down my cheeks. My thoughts were also with the fallen soldiers who never got to experience this day – Mikkel, Thorbjørn, Anders, Mark and Casper – and with our many wounded soldiers.

'We did it. We actually freed our area from the Taliban.'

It was a sentence I repeated to myself many times. I thought the worst was over, and that I and my soldiers would soon be on our way home to our families in Denmark.

The following night I slept deeply and well, waking with a fantastic feeling in my body. After eating breakfast and enjoying the sun, which was already high in the sky, I lay down to get a bit more rest before returning to our main base in Gereshk.

In the late morning, I suddenly heard yelling and shouting coming from outside Sandford's thick clay walls. I thought, 'They're playing football. I'm so glad I got to experience that too – someone must have scored a goal.'

Ten minutes later I was shaken out of my doze when the company's second-in-command came running over towards my camp-bed with a shocked look on his face.

'Did you hear that racket outside?' he shouted.

'Yes, is something wrong?' I asked.

'There was a mob of angry people claiming we burned a Koran!'

He told me he had been called up to the main sentry post because a large crowd of people had gathered. A platoon had been given orders to put on their combat gear and come too.

Outside were seventy or eighty furious Afghans screaming and shouting. One of the company's local interpreters translated the tirade. The demonstrators claimed that

Danish soldiers had blasphemed against the sacred book by throwing it onto a bonfire. One held 'proof' in his hands: a Koran singed on one side. Another accusation was that Danish soldiers had relieved themselves in a mosque.

The company's second-in-command had explained that naturally we would never do such a thing. After a while the Afghans trickled away, but not before emphasising their anger by spitting and throwing stones, and the ringleaders shouted a phrase that was echoed by the mob in a rather disquieting way. To the soldiers it sounded like a curse.

I could hardly have had a more rude awakening.

'That's a total lie,' I thought. 'We've just got rid of the Taliban and the very next day we've got our own Mohammed-related crisis on our hands.'

I knew that the situation was volatile. If the crisis wasn't handled quickly and effectively, things could go badly wrong. Right now, it was impossible to know what the demonstrators had in mind. Would they return with 2,000 men before the day was out? Would the whole Green Zone be on the warpath the next morning? What would happen in the town of Gereshk?

I only managed to exchange a few words with the company's second-in-command before I heard a sudden uproar at the end of the camp, where a platoon from the Afghan army, ANA, was quartered.

We had twenty-five or thirty Afghan (ANA) soldiers with us, there to learn from the Danish and British soldiers, and we from them.

We never determined exactly what happened but, fundamentally, there were only two possibilities: either the

Afghan interpreter ran directly from the main guardhouse to the approximately thirty ANA soldiers to tell them that the Danes had been accused of burning a Koran, or he ran directly over to the ANA soldiers to tell them that the Danes *had* burned a Koran.

In any case, the response was violent. The Afghan soldiers lost all control. They put on combat gear and helmets, aiming their weapons and rocket-propelled grenades at the nearest Danes, while they shouted threateningly.

We were on the verge of chaos. Everybody could feel it. The Danish and British soldiers in the camp also quickly put on their combat gear, and the entrance to the Afghan part of the camp was put under surveillance. The atmosphere became increasingly intense on both sides, so I knew I had to act quickly.

My biggest fear was that someone would overreact. If even a single shot was fired it would almost certainly be followed by 300, 500 or 1,000 more, and when the smoke cleared there would be casualties on both sides.

A conflict over the Koran that took less than an hour to escalate into a bloodbath in which Danish, British and Afghan soldiers killed each other inside a camp would make international headlines, and the consequences would be incalculable.

In another situation, I would have tried to analyse what to do, weighing up the pros and cons of different solutions before I took a decision, but there wasn't time to do that here. I looked to my intuition. I see intuition more as an instinctive feeling than an analytical process. My feeling was that I had to do something, and I had to do it now!

I took a few steps forward. Then I took off my helmet and combat gear and put my gun down on the sand. Unarmed and without any kind of protection, I walked across the open space directly towards the agitated Afghans, who were pointing their weapons at me.

'Where are you going?' I heard my bodyguard shout. I didn't turn around, but signalled with my hand for him to stay where he was. My idea was to create a moment's confusion and try to take back the initiative by doing what the Afghan soldiers least expected. I now had to use this moment of surprise to assert myself. So I stopped right in front of them and spoke:

I see intuition more as an instinctive feeling than an analytical process.

'I'm standing here in front of you unarmed. Let me ask you this: what kind of situation are we getting ourselves into? We've fought together against the Taliban. Are we now going to start killing each other? When false accusations were made against us a little while ago, I thought: it's a good thing we have ANA soldiers among us, so they can help us clear up this misunderstanding. We would never burn a Koran. How could you think that of us? Now I expect you to join us in finding a solution to the problem that has arisen.'

The surprise had an effect on some, but unfortunately not all, the Afghan soldiers. One sergeant walked threateningly towards me and slammed his rifle into the ground in front of me with all his might. Four or five of his comrades tried to whip up the atmosphere still further. But I could tell from making eye contact with the unit that most of them were uncomfortable with the tense situation, and after a little while they began to regain some of their composure.

I went back to my armoured personnel carrier and thought through what had just occurred: had I been nervous and afraid when I walked unarmed and unprotected up to the furious Afghans?

No – in the moment I was perfectly serene, even with the risk of being shot. I was completely concentrated and focused. Whatever happened, happened.

But afterwards, as I sat in my armoured vehicle, my body gave way. Nervousness crept in somehow, getting under my skin. We had been a hair's breadth away from being finished. I had experienced the same sensation during the mission in the Balkans: you feel as though you've aged several years in just a few minutes.

If I hadn't intervened, I'm convinced to this day that the volatile situation in the camp would have exploded, and we would have had a nightmare on our hands. My intuition helped me to exercise 'here-and-now' leadership.

Many others before me have been through the same thing: having to take decisions without adequate time or information. I have been fascinated by the phenomenon ever since I was a young cadet at the Royal Danish Military Academy in Frederiksberg Palace. Stories about military leaders who chose to follow their gut at decisive moments, who defied experts' advice to find an alternative solution and stood firm, eventually succeeding, gave me plenty of food for thought. As we sat in the lecture hall, learning about the military theorist Carl von Clausewitz, Napoleon or generals like George Patton and Erich von Manstein, my imagination ran riot.

At that point I didn't understand the depths of intuitive leadership. It requires a stockpile of experiences, stored in your brain layer by layer, so that later you can pull them out and draw on the power of intuition at crucial moments. But I tried to picture myself in situations where I had to trust my gut instead of simply relying on the far more demanding analytical work, and I am convinced that – as far as that goes – you are profoundly shaped by lessons in history.

Carl von Clausewitz (1780–1831) studied over 130 campaigns, was himself an active participant in warfare and encountered Napoleon, among other people, first hand. Later on, he wrote several books about his experiences and reflections, which are compulsory reading for every officer, and much of what he had to say is equally relevant for people outside the military, in industry and elsewhere. Clausewitz emphasises that when you're commanding a unit during wartime, you cannot let your actions be dictated purely by restrictions, directives and guidelines. He is a staunch opponent of those devoted to systems. When chaos reigns, systems must give way to the leader's feeling for warfare. He must recognise that not everything can be orchestrated according to a mathematical formula, relying instead on his intuition and judgement.

A successful leader has excellent grounding in the form of historical insight, and he is present – both physically and mentally – in the heat of battle. He looks ahead so as to respond promptly in the worst situations he can imagine, but he must also be ready to accept and act on the consequences of a flash of insight.

That was what I experienced during the ANA soldiers' violent outburst.

At the moment I realised that things might go badly wrong, my body reacted in a peculiar way. I was like an air-tight bubble, with sounds, sensations and impressions suddenly whirling around at grotesquely high speed. As I walked towards the armed ANA soldiers, it was as if all the experiences and impressions I had stockpiled from similar episodes I had heard about, or experienced myself, came back to me with fierce intensity. I was thinking that an officer mustn't let anybody down. I was picturing headlines in the papers and news anchors on TV talking about a bloodbath involving Danish, English and Afghan soldiers in Helmand. I saw myself being shot, and wondering whether it was worth it.

A successful leader has excellent grounding in the form of historical insight, and he is present – both physically and mentally – in the heat of battle.

Words whizzed through my brain: 'Surprise, surprise, surprise – you have to surprise the ANA soldiers so you can get a few seconds of their attention before they start shooting.' I was thinking, too: *for God's sake, you have to have the first sentences ready when the moment comes to speak.* The lines formed in my mind almost of their own accord.

I could keep describing it word for word and image by image. I was juggling an absurdly high number of impressions in the few seconds I had to figure out what to do.

When I look back on that situation, I don't see how I could have managed it in such a short space of time. In an analytical process and under normal circumstances it would have taken a very long time to get there. I also don't understand the clarity with which I instinctively made that decision. It was as if every piece of this tsunami of information helped me to make sense of the situation and do what had to be done in that moment.

Once it was all behind us, naturally, the relieved crowd of soldiers had plenty of questions. 'Why did you do it? Why did you take off all your combat gear? How did you know they wouldn't shoot you?'

The only answer I could offer was: 'It came to me.'

There's no direct logical explanation, but haven't we all – to a greater or lesser extent – fallen back on our intuition in pressured situations and thought afterwards: 'What happened just then? How did I just know that that was the right thing to do in the moment?'

In my conversations with businesspeople, sportsmen and -women and artists, I have found that they all put this experience into more or less the same words.

They draw on something different – and deeper – than what their rational minds suggest. Personally, I'm in no doubt that intuition is reinforced by history and experience, and therefore also previous analytical work. 'Prepare your mind', as they say. It's about storing information on the brain's hard disk. That's how it works.

But when we get that flash of insight, giving us an over-all picture in a split-second, and we can act at lightning speed, something else is going on. If we were to analyse the complex problem rationally and logically, we would break it up into smaller pieces, examine them individually and put them back together again. Time would be a decisive factor. We would be unable to solve the problem, face the challenge or avoid danger in the moment. We therefore have to base these crucial deci-sions and assessments on intui-tion, gut feeling and emotion.

The human brain is massively powerful, and this power does not necessarily have to be brought to bear through an analytical approach. Remarkably, it can assess, judge and prioritise in a split-second – and it can do so without a deliberate and closely reasoned mechanical analysis.

Personally, I'm in no doubt that intuition is reinforced by history and experience.

When it comes to the crunch, you are able to draw on information stored deep inside your brain. This has been my experience. I have been helped by my intuition when I was really under pressure. I wonder whether stock traders, racing drivers, surgeons, politicians and people in many other professions feel the same way?

The next question that arises is naturally: how do we engage day-to-day with something that isn't analytical or precisely quantifiable? After all, it's difficult to take exams in a sub-ject that's all about gut feeling in the here and now. And I imagine that very few people have been taught, trained and tested for their ability to listen to their intuition in everyday life, whether in the military or in their company, board or department.

And yet, I would claim that during my training as an officer I did in fact learn something about taking intuition, gut feeling and emotion very seriously. I just didn't realise it at the time.

I must also admit that when I taught at the Royal Danish Military Academy, I didn't put 'developing your intuition' on the formal curriculum. But, today it is clear to me that what I saw young leaders achieve during the war in Helmand was integrally connected to the training they received. They had to listen closely to their intuition. Nearly every day they found themselves in situations where there was no time for analysis, deep thought or reflection. Commanding thirty or a hundred soldiers under constant fire, they had to draw on experiences stored deep within their brains to successfully achieve their objectives.

What deliberate training had they undertaken at the Army Non-Commissioned Officer School or the military academy? What deeply ingrained leadership tools had they acquired in the Balkans, Africa, Iraq or elsewhere? Can you really train yourself to rely more on your intuition?

I want to draw a parallel with Chapter 3, where I wrote that in certain situations it's better to take three decisions you're 80% happy with than one that's 100% perfect. When, as a leader, you have to act under chaotic circumstances, nothing will ever go 100% as planned. There is constant uncertainty, and something always happens to make even the most brilliant plan fall apart.

In the military world you are at constant risk of being shot, and sometimes soldiers are wounded or killed. A young sergeant's training will reflect this so that, when things don't go according to plan, he is prepared for the worst. In a sense, he will be trained to worry about everything that might go wrong, gradually storing up information and experiences in his brain. If things do go wrong, he's mentally prepared.

Later in his career, the sergeant or officer will have stored up thousands of situations where he didn't find a 100% perfect solution. He has done constant drills where he had to be okay with putting a plan into action despite his information base being 40 or 60% incomplete. To compensate for this lack of information and the chaos that arises from it, he has to rely on his intuition.

When a young leader has been in a touch-and-go situation, where his life was on the line, and yet he still achieved his objective with flying colours, he often explains afterwards: 'I felt it was the only right thing to do in that situation.'

But what about future leaders who have a university background in law or finance, or a business-related discipline? To what extent are they trained to have a '40 or 60%' approach, as outlined above? There is no doubt that we will desperately need creative and innovative solutions in industry and government going forward, but have we trained our future leaders to think outside the box, beyond the purely analytical or rational? Have we also remembered to take intuition into account? Do we support them in daring to rely on their gut when it comes to doing the right thing, or are we pushing them towards the notion that there *must* always be a logical, analytical and closely reasoned answer?

It takes courage and self-confidence to follow your intuition, especially when the stakes are high and everybody around you has a different solution in mind. This kind of self-confidence only comes from being tested as a leader and experiencing for yourself that it works. Today, I don't doubt it for a second – not least after having witnessed the unique leadership shown by young officers during wartime. At the Royal Danish Military Academy and in practical training we have built up their self-confidence and the belief that they can lead by intuition, even if they would probably call it something else.

There is no doubt that we will desperately need creative and innovative solutions in industry and government going forward, but have we trained our future leaders to think outside the box, beyond the purely analytical or rational?

I am certain that intuition-based decision-making is especially prevalent among leaders in critical situations, where they have to act in the here and now. In those situations, you really become aware of the power of intuition.

As mentioned above, this phenomenon is also found outside the military – in the sciences, for instance. The atomic physicist Niels Bohr discovered that insights can come to you in a split second, as all of a sudden you see the whole picture. In 1939, with other researchers at Princeton University, he was discussing the risks of splitting the atom. At one point, the other researchers were afraid Bohr had had a stroke: he leaned forward until his head was resting against the table. After a while, he suddenly exclaimed: 'There will be a chain reaction if you split uranium 235 and bombard it with neutrons.' A few hours later he produced a mathematical proof of his claim. When asked by the other researchers how he had suddenly arrived at that realisation, he could only reply that it had come to him.

I feel that I've got to know my intuition better over time. There's no doubt that it has been an invaluable resource during difficult missions, but I have also had to work on learning to accept that it is worth following – especially when something important is at stake.

Reaching the inner state I need in order to get the most of my intuition has been a personal challenge for me. I like having things under control and knowing that I have a detailed plan in place, but over the years I have become better at taking a step back and letting that last decisive per cent be determined by circumstance. In my current job as Master of Ceremonies I am aware that 'chaos' will – to a certain extent – reign when we are on a state visit, a cruise on the royal yacht or at an ambassadorial reception.

As I say to my closest colleagues: 'The bigger the unforeseen problems that arise, the more we smile. Nobody else knows how things were supposed to go – only we know that – so smile, for goodness' sake. That way we'll be much better placed to face the challenges that come our way.'

I do try to minimise chaos, of course, but something unexpected always crops up. Now, having reached that realisation – and being aware of it – I can actively welcome intuition. And that's exactly what happens. I have confidence in myself; I know I can 'lead the charge', and that whatever will happen will happen, one way or another.

I accept that there won't necessarily be a logical explanation for why it happens. In some situations I can simply feel intuition taking over, as everything accelerates to a breakneck speed and images, impressions, answers and warnings wash over me – and I just accept this for what it is.

In my younger days, I could end up wandering speechlessly around by myself when this sensation struck. One day in 1995, as the Croatians and Serbs waged war with each other and the conflict intensified in my area of responsibility, I was giving orders to my units over the radio; thousands of feelings were rushing through me, when I suddenly had an insight: 'We won't get hurt – nothing's going to happen to us – nobody's going to be killed.'

Although the battle raged on, I turned around, looked at the officers and sergeants standing around me, and said in a loud, clear voice: 'We won't get hurt – nothing's going to happen to us – nobody's going to be killed.'

They goggled at me. What did the commander just say? How could he know that, when we were in the middle of a battle? I was also a bit shaken by what I'd said – in fact, I didn't feel like I was the person who'd said it. It just slipped out.

'I don't know why I said that, but I can tell you that nothing is going to happen to us,' was the only answer I could give them.

Was it my intuition that 'came to me', or was this based on something else?

I believe it was my intuition, similar to the confrontation with the ANA soldiers. Suddenly – in the middle of intense combat – the same tidal wave of experiences, knowledge, feelings and images came flooding over me. I sensed the 'rhythm of the battle', the duration of the individual encounter and, indeed, the whole atmosphere. And it just slipped out: 'We won't get hurt.'

Obviously, that's one of the silliest things you can say as a commander while the battle is in full flow. I myself was surprised over the sudden flash of clarity. I don't know where it came from, but I was absolutely sure. We weren't going to get hurt!

Has my intuition ever let me down? Yes, it has. It didn't in Krajina, thank God, or during the incident with the ANA soldiers, but I have been in other situations where I hoped it would guide me – when I had to decide whether the tanks should drive over the bridge in Gereshk, for instance – but it turned out to be no help at all. Bloody intuition – just when I needed it, it fell silent.

The times when I have felt alone as a leader, having to make weighty decisions, it has been a great help to say a prayer and hope that it's heard. I feel it gives me a sense of inner calm, and calm is everything for a leader responsible for the lives of other human beings – in war as in life. If you do nothing else, you should project a sense of calm.

On my chest are tattooed the words 'Dominus provide-bit'. It was Frederick III's royal motto, and it means 'The Lord will provide'. It's also the motto of the 1st Company in the Royal Lifeguards – the unit I myself have commanded twice, and the unit deployed on the front lines in the fight against the Taliban in the autumn of 2007. It's an eternal reminder to myself that God will help and support me during even the most difficult trials, giving me the calm I need when things go wrong.

Other leaders will have something else that works for them. I have excellent colleagues who meditate or use physical exercise as part of their preparations. Others listen to music. It's actually rather surprising how different we all are in that regard. But one thing is clear to me: nearly all of us have something or other we rely on. For me, it has been necessary to believe in something greater, something that supports me. This isn't necessarily better than anything else, but it's been of tremendous help to me.

When, as a leader, I have been unsure about a decision I have been forced to take – i.e. a decision that might cost human lives – I have always operated according to the following fundamental rule: if in doubt, listen to your brain and your heart. If they agree, then there's no debate. If they don't, then listen to your heart.

You know in your heart whether you will be able to live with yourself for the rest of your life if you take a particular decision. Several times, I have taken a decision to say no to something, even though from an analytical, rational perspective it seemed like I ought to say yes. This is true in work-related business and personal matters and, indeed, also in an operative context.

If you are about to take a decision that sets in motion something that breaks your heart, then my advice is this: find another solution.

On various courses, and in other contexts, I have spoken to industry leaders about the dangers of clinging to the rational and the objective when your intuition is guiding you in another direction. It takes courage to follow your heart, especially when you have a board of directors or shareholders demanding clear answers about everything.

If in doubt, listen to your brain and your heart. If they agree, then there's no debate. If they don't, then listen to your heart.

The pressure you feel as a leader is greatest when you are responsible for other people who themselves are facing severe challenges. This is why the next chapter focuses on something very important: you will never be successful as a leader if your employees don't feel that you are on their side – that you are considerate towards them and willing to lift the burden from their shoulders.

CHAPTER 7

Love Your Employees

ON 8 AUGUST 1995 I was standing at one of our outposts in Krajina with my arms around a staff sergeant. Tears were running down our cheeks.

'I'm finished as an officer,' I was thinking. 'How can my soldiers continue to have confidence in me and follow me when I'm standing here crying?'

The hostilities around the Croatian offensive were gradually beginning to ease off, and after many months' uncertainty and the previous days' fierce fighting things were nearing an end.

The Danish outpost was one that had been particularly badly affected by the Croatian bombardment. Shells had literally rained down on them, because Serbian units were encamped either side of the outpost. Since it was also an area the Croatians had to control in order to continue their attack, the whole situation rapidly deteriorated into pure hell for my soldiers.

They hadn't slept for more than four days – it was impossible, because the conflict might at any moment cause them to be killed or wounded – so they were on the brink of exhaustion when I reached them.

The staff sergeant came over towards me at once. He only managed to tell me how important it had been for him to be able to hear my voice over the radio the whole time before the tears welled up. He was one of the sergeants I most valued, and I knew that the responsibility for his unit had weighed heavily on his shoulders. Now the pressure had been lifted, and I could see he felt a tremendous sense of relief – as, indeed, did I – that nobody in our company had been wounded or killed.

It was impossible to hold back the tears, but as I stood there in the middle of the outpost with my arms around the staff sergeant, all the others soldiers' eyes upon us, I couldn't help feeling embarrassed. How could they ever respect me as a commander after seeing that?

What happened? To my great astonishment, the response was unambiguous: for the soldiers it was an extremely powerful moment. They knew we had both been working day and night to look after them, and they took the hug as an expression of our relief that nobody had been hurt.

On a mission, you're with other people twenty-four hours a day for six months. You never really have a moment to yourself, so you can't be anything other than, well, yourself. If you try to put on a pretence, at some point you'll be found out. You can't act like you're Rambo for a whole six months. Sooner or later, your true colours will be revealed.

In Krajina I made a virtue of visiting all the outposts once a day, insofar as that was possible. It became a daily routine to go and talk to the soldiers, sharing funny experiences and listening to their concerns. We became close – as the intensity of the conflict increased – and I came to care about them deeply.

Many people have tried to convince me that I get too involved. But I simply cannot help it. I was their commander, and it was my responsibility to do everything in my power to look after my soldiers and bring them home in good shape. I felt like a big brother or a father to them – I would even go so far as to say that I loved the soldiers on those missions.

Did I really love them? It's one thing to love your children or your family, but can you also love your soldiers and colleagues?

Yes, I do mean it seriously, even though it elicits plenty of sceptical questions when I give lectures, and at first glance you might think it's a bit over the top. I use the word 'love' deliberately, just in another sense than the one in which parents love their children – although perhaps that too, actually. My point is that love is integral to performance at the highest level.

'You should treat your soldiers as if they were your own children. If you do that, they will follow you through even the deepest valleys,' wrote the Chinese general, military strategist and philosopher Sun Tzu around 500 BCE.

How far can we, must we and may we go as leaders in viewing employees like our own children – and in showing them the care and affection that entails? Think it over, because I have found that it can provide fodder for many productive hours of discussion.

I myself have taken up the challenge, trying to unpick this fundamental question: 'Why are soldiers (or employees in general) willing to follow their leaders through fire and water in order to excel?'

My answer is that not even the biggest raise, the best bonus or the most dramatic career shift can make an employee risk their own life by walking out into a hail of bullets – either literally or figuratively. That only happens if, ultimately, they have faith in the leader standing in front of them. And that's all about love!

My answer is that not even the biggest raise, the best bonus or the most dramatic career shift can make an employee risk their own life by walking out into a hail of bullets – either literally or figuratively.

When you're given responsibility for soldiers, this brings with it certain other duties. You can't – or at least I can't – help thinking of their loved-ones. If their loved-ones don't have confidence in you as a leader, the soldiers will never find the sense of calm they need to deal with the extraordinary challenges of warfare.

If they're under heavy pressure on the home front, they will lose focus, becoming a danger to themselves and others.

As a commander during wartime, I took responsibility for the thing most precious to any soldier's family – a father, a mother, a brother, a sister, a husband or a wife. If I hadn't always behaved in a way that made it clear to everybody involved that I was concerned about them, then I'd have had problems. Who would support their beloved son or daughter setting off on a dangerous mission if they saw the commander as an unreliable and untrustworthy cynic? Nobody, of course. Soldiers' loved-ones have to believe that the commander cares about his people's lives.

This is a particular challenge when we're talking about soldiers during a time of war. Their loved-ones will naturally be frightened and anxious – every single day. But if they also find the commander callous, things can easily go wrong.

Of course, the problem isn't quite as pressing day-to-day in an ordinary company, but it's still highly relevant. You shouldn't underestimate how much employees are affected by their loved-ones' attitude towards their workplace and their boss. It has a big impact, so they *must* fundamentally feel confident that the boss wants the best for his or her employees.

When you show an interest in your employees, as well as consideration and respect, you create a strong foundation to work from; but it takes more than that for them to follow you through fire and water. This is where leadership becomes truly challenging.

In 1998, a book was published that I have read many times over, because it always gives me food for thought: *The Servant*, by James C. Hunter. The book has been a great source of inspiration for me, as it's about how leaders should try to be themselves while maintaining high ethical standards – basically, about how to behave properly and decently in all contexts. This isn't always easy. You try to do your best, and it doesn't always come off – but trying is at least a step in the right direction.

The book is about a businessman called John Daily, whose life is starting to fall apart. He's having terrible trouble at work, at his sports club and at home, and his wife is pressuring him to take a week off to think things over. John goes on a retreat at a Benedictine monastery, where he attends seminars given by the monks. One of them used to be a top executive at one of the USA's largest corporations, before leaving the business world and devoting his life to God.

At one point, the course participants are asked to think about what qualities they most prize about the leader they consider their biggest role model – whether that's a boss, a coach, a teacher or even their mother, for that matter. Why would they be willing to stick with that person through thick and thin? What makes that leader unique?

John Daily has never really reflected much on his leadership style. His thoughts touch on many different people – including his mother – and he realises that, ultimately, what's important is that a leader is there for others, always steps up, is never judgemental and pays attention when people speak.

During the process, he is also reminded of how difficult he must be as a boss. He never listens, instead cutting people off when they're trying to get something off their chest. He's always getting into disputes with trade unions or employees, and is forced to admit that he never shows any kind of consideration or interest in them. Not trusting his employees, he's always breathing down their necks.

John Daily leaves the monastery with a much more humble perspective on what it means to be a leader, and is determined to be a better husband, too – one who doesn't put himself first.

Read the book and be inspired.

Qualities like honesty and trustworthiness, the ability to listen and be caring, to encourage and motivate people and to be passionate – these are all things that are highlighted on 'top ten' lists of the world's best leaders. It's not about paying higher salaries or distributing bigger bonuses, but about the ability to create relationships with your employees, showing trust in them instead of controlling them and falling back on rigid discipline.

None of this is a sign of weakness. Quite the opposite, actually: it's hard to imagine a more demanding kind of leadership. Daring to allow yourself to become deeply involved is challenging for any leader. Strict, unyielding discipline is much easier.

What would your own list look like? How would you want your boss to be? My guess is that you'd come up with a list of qualities very similar to the one above.

Qualities like honesty and trustworthiness, the ability to listen and be caring, to encourage and motivate people and to be passionate – these are all things that are highlighted on 'top ten' lists of the world's best leaders.

And here's my next question: what consequences does that have for your own style of leadership? If those are the qualities you value in a leader, wouldn't it be good to try and operate according to the same principles?

If you do, you will most likely be exercising 'servant leadership' – which we might also term 'inclusive leadership'.

It's a philosophy of leadership that can be traced back to another Chinese thinker, Lao-Tzu, who lived around the same time as Sun Tzu, and its message is essentially that the greatest leaders are actually servants of the people. They aren't driven by a personal lust for power, but by a genuine wish to serve their followers, so that they become freer, healthier, wiser and happier people. You can also find this philosophy in the major religious texts – in the Gospel According to Mark, for instance (10:43–45): 'whosoever will be great among you, shall be your minister: And

173

whosoever of you will be the chiefest, shall be servant of all. For even the Son of man came not to be ministered unto, but to minister, and to give his life a ransom for many.'

For me, servant leadership is about the ability to listen and be empathetic, and about the desire to give encouragement, support and development of employees the highest priority, so that they can fulfil their potential.

Soldiers aren't there for the officers. It's the other way around. The officers are there for the soldiers.

As the Guard Hussars put it: first the horses, then the troops and finally yourself. This speaks volumes.

If, as a leader, you operate according to that principle, there's a good chance that your employees will be there for you. And you need your employees – perhaps most of all when you're really hard-pressed.

I have always made sure to find soldiers who would support, understand and protect me. As a commander during wartime you're very exposed, and it's been an invaluable help for me to have employees who 'looked after' me.

Soldiers aren't there for the officers. It's the other way around. The officers are there for the soldiers.

One person who has always been there for me over the years is Per. A born soldier and a true professional, he has been by my side since 1989, always attentive to my state of mind or the dangers I might encounter. During the incident when I walked unarmed up to the agitated ANA soldiers in Afghanistan to try to calm things down, he quickly found out that I had 'gone off somewhere'. A few minutes later he'd found me and was standing by my side again.

One afternoon, after an intense bout of fighting in which one of our soldiers had been killed, I was sitting in my armoured personnel carrier and feeling utterly at my wits' end. I was tired, worn out and deeply affected by the loss we had suffered. When soldiers lose their lives, we write to their bereaved relatives. But where do you draw the line? Should you write a letter to a two-year-old and a six-year-old whose father has been killed? That was what was running through my mind as I sat there that afternoon, and I alone could make the decision.

I tried to begin the letter several times, but I could only manage a single line before the tears began to run down my cheeks so heavily that writing was impossible. I simply couldn't, even though I wanted to.

I could feel Per looking at me from a distance. Suddenly, he was standing in front of me, crouching down and giving me a big hug as he whispered into my ear:

'It's not always much fun being in charge. Shall I make you a cup of coffee?'

'Thanks, Per, that would be nice.'

Per didn't just make coffee for me that day. He also made sure to keep other people out of the way so that I could write the letters in peace. He told everybody who wanted to talk to me that I was busy, but that they could have a cup of coffee while they waited.

His attitude towards me and everyone else was enormously important to the unit. I can only recommend in the strongest possible terms that you identify your own 'Per' within your company and bond with him.

Servant leadership is therefore about loving your employees – in the sense that you should be patient, friendly, humble, respectful and forgiving in everything you do. In doing so, you ensure loyal employees, ones who – like Per – will always stick up for you when you need it.

This doesn't mean that you shouldn't also lay down ground-rules and hold employees accountable. That mustn't be neglected. I'm not advocating for leading as if you're giving a therapy session, with everybody sitting in a circle and holding hands while they agree on everything. It's hard to find a balance. When should you get involved, and when should you take full responsibility as a leader and map out a course?

I'm afraid you can't find the answer in a spreadsheet or a form where you tick off boxes. It takes practice, practice and more practice.

It's also important to think about the responsibility that comes with leadership. No matter what leadership role you hold, you are responsible for other people. You have direct influence over their everyday lives, as it's the person immediately in charge who has the greatest impact on the welfare of those working for them. But your responsibility goes further than that, beyond individual employees: you also play an important role for your employees' families. As a leader, you will be scrutinised and discussed over the kitchen table, and the judgements made there will affect your employees' attitude at work and their desire to perform day-to-day.

Remember: *everything* you do as a leader will be observed by your employees. Your mood, your facial expressions, your demeanour – *everything* is observed, noted and stored in their memory banks. If you are also able to take an interest in your employees' relatives and to be concerned on their behalf when issues arise, then you are a boss who has the energy it takes to succeed in the long run.

Assuming this responsibility is a demanding process. Things don't always work. You'll make mistakes, you'll make a fool of yourself, and you'll have to try again – and hopefully it'll go a little smoother next time. The important thing is to decide that you *want* to exercise 'servant' or inclusive leadership instead of controlling leadership. If you do, I promise you that you'll get the performance and the results you're looking for further down the line.

> Remember: *everything you do as a leader will be observed by your employees.*

Note that I make a distinction between performance and results. The essence of good leadership is to maintain a consistent focus on performance, which should be improved on every day. You do need to look at the cold, hard facts of how your results measure up, but this shouldn't be the decisive factor during the day-to-day grind. The crucial thing is your employees' performance day after day – whether at the production plant, the firing range or university lecture theatres.

It is in striving each day to optimise performance – bearing in mind the overall goal – that talented leaders can be inspirational and motivating.

If you rise up through the ranks, climbing the ladder and earning stars on your shoulder, it's very important to remember the rungs below you. Everything you do as a leader must be comprehensible to your employees and practically applicable to their everyday activities. You will have an advantage in that regard if you yourself have worked in the engine room, or if you are at least interested enough in the working conditions there to find out what they're like.

I've mentioned this already, but you have got to respect the basic working conditions of your employees and the 'little things' necessary for them to perform. Think back to my story about the dead light bulb. It's a cautionary tale for all leaders, and I use it as a powerful reminder that, from time to time, we have to drag our attention away from our own brilliance and focus on the essentials.

In 1996, as a company commander with the Lifeguards, where I was responsible for more than 150 soldiers, I was taught a lesson by an old hand who wasn't afraid to talk back to the boss. I held weekly meetings with representatives from the individual units to give a run-down of what had been happening, and to talk about how things had gone and what to expect going forward. I was keen to keep people in the loop about everything that was going on, big and small – probably mostly big, if I'm being honest – in and around our unit. I spoke about political issues in a broad international context and about how we fitted into the larger picture and, on the whole, I was satisfied with my performance as a leader. Privately, I thought I was doing the representatives a favour by spending all that time giving an explanation about the overarching strategy of which we were a part.

After a few weeks of feeling pleased with myself, I was taken aside by one of the older and more experienced staff sergeants, who had administrative responsibility for the unit. Did I have a few minutes?

The staff sergeant was generally precise and no-nonsense in the way he expressed himself, and this occasion was no exception. He just wanted to know whether, in the upcoming meetings with the representatives, I was intending to continue to lecture them about broad-brush issues in Danish foreign and security policy, and about things going on in the Danish military, the Lifeguards and our battalion more generally?

I sensed that he wasn't in favour of this idea. Instead, he suggested I try paying more attention to the problems the representatives kept bringing up, for instance, that there was a nagging shortage of light bulbs in the barracks and bathrooms.

Well there you go! Welcome to the real world! There I was, thinking that my elegant analyses would please and satisfy my soldiers, and all the while the issue most important to them was that they couldn't see beyond the end of their noses in the barracks. I quickly set 'operation light bulb' in motion and the problem was resolved.

Thanks for the reminder, sergeant! You have no idea how many times I've thought of you when confronted with the mundane problems I'd prefer to forget because I'm so preoccupied with the bigger picture.

It's the little things you're judged on as a leader – never forget that! If you find yourself in a similar situation, turn your hearing aid up to eleven. Listen intently, write things down and set about fixing the problem at once. That way you show respect and understanding for the issues your employees are grappling with, the ones which get in the way of all the good ideas you'd like to have them on board with.

Sort out the bulbs – get the lights working – and then tell them about your grand strategic plan.

Let me emphasise that I'm talking here about solving very real and pressing issues that cause problems in everyday life. I don't mean that as leaders we should do anything and everything employees try and wheedle us into. This is a misunderstanding I come across from time to time when I'm giving lectures on leadership – that employees should be the ones really in control of the company's actions.

I want to make it clear that it's the leader's responsibility to choose a course and forge ahead. It's the leader who has the ultimate, definitive power to fire and hire people, and the corresponding dynamism to inspire, motivate and care for his or her employees.

I keep using the word 'care'. It has positive associations, of course, but for me it also contains an important nuance. Previously, I described the rigorous training that we instituted before the Afghanistan mission. We did so with the soldiers' wellbeing in mind, but I can't say that at the time it was perceived as soft and cuddly – indeed, this was an occasion where we really had to crack the whip. The greatest care you can show your soldiers is to train them as hard as possible prior to the mission. There's no guarantee that they will love you at the time, but they'll be grateful when they get home in one piece.

Other people use terms like 'tough love', and that's exactly what I'm talking about. You shouldn't be afraid to make demands on people. You genuinely want your employees to be as capable as possible, and this means creating a balance between the caring, touchy-feely stuff on the one hand and a friendly kick up the backside or dull, frustrating exercises on the other.

I want to make it clear that it's the leader's responsibility to choose a course and forge ahead. It's the leader who has the ultimate, definitive power to fire and hire people, and the corresponding dynamism to inspire, motivate and care for his or her employees.

Finding this balance can be difficult. Neither is it easy to know how closely you should get involved when being caring towards an employee. For some leaders, even asking about an employee's family can feel like crossing a line, and there are definitely some employees who prefer to maintain a certain distance from their boss.

But I believe that it is on this superlative form of leadership – high-performance leadership – that countries should set their sights. Future leaders should be capable of being both gentle and tough, and of getting involved with people on an individual level. They should function like catalysts, filtering and translating strategies and objectives into meaningful challenges that speak to employees' personal ambitions and augment their desire to perform at a high level.

Future leaders should be able to recruit, develop and hold onto the most talented employees. Future employees will expect involved and service-orientated leaders.

When the CEO of Lego, Jørgen Vig Knudstorp, almost dancing for joy over another fantastic set of accounts, said that their 'success was due to thousands of people having done a huge amount of work I hadn't asked them to do', you don't need much imagination to be able to work out what brought the company such tremendous success: I think individual employees were given the space they needed to carry out their work well.

Let me take a quick detour. If you've reached the point where you love your employees almost as if they were your own children and you see the company as your family, what consequences might that have for your own, actual family? How do you make sure they don't pay a high price for your dedication as a leader, if you are absent and your focus is elsewhere? In other words: how do you find a reasonable balance between your work life and your family life?

Over the last ten years I have had the opportunity to spend time with many successful, very senior leaders, and to discuss this very question in confidence. One thing all of them have in common is that their working day is not nine to five. They're available 24/7. Although they do often try to tone down the degree to which they engage with their work, the reality is that they are married to their jobs.

Is it different for successful officials, officers, sports stars or cultural figures? No. In my experience they also feel a sense of responsibility that takes up a lot of their energy.

Every once in a while you hear about 'superleaders' who say that they're able to balance their private and professional lives perfectly. I can't help cracking a smile and thinking to myself that they're probably lying. Certainly, I don't know anybody who could say that hand on heart.

I'm also aware from personal experience that a leadership role in which you have ultimate responsibility for employees who are expected to give their very best demands a massive amount of your day-to-day energy and attention. There are certain periods where I have to be 'on' twenty-four hours a day. Not all year round, of course, but when I really have to excel as a leader, as in Afghanistan in 2007–08, for instance. During that period, the training, the mission itself, returning home and winding things down afterwards was *everything*!

'Sure, but my work is also my hobby.' Have you heard that one before?

I have! And I have also met leaders, especially in the world of sports and the arts, who really are living the dream. The extraordinary performances at the Royal Ballet, for instance, only come from passionate full-time leadership. I don't doubt that for a second.

But can't that turn into sheer hell? And isn't it incredibly stressful for employees to have a boss who works on a project 24/7?

This is certainly something we have to take seriously. Focusing unthinkingly on meeting objectives and constantly pushing yourself to work quickly is unhealthy. So think twice before jumping into everything at once as a leader, and give yourself a chance to consider various priorities, frameworks, working conditions and resources.

In striving to get the best out of your talented employees, you have a duty to keep an eye on their welfare, minimising stress and boosting their personal development.

This brings us back to the framework in which employees and managers operate, and here I want to sound a warning bell: in my experience, over the last ten or fifteen years we have seen a tremendous amount of energy sunk into regulation, controls and performance targets.

Haven't we all known bosses who say yes to everything almost automatically, without taking their staff into account? I certainly have – and it creates stress.

On the other hand, I have rarely heard of bosses being turned away empty-handed if they go to their immediate superiors with a good argument for why they lack the resources (financial, material or staff-related) to carry out this or that project. No, the danger lies in bosses who don't initiate that conversation.

I have found that being sensible about how you prioritise your and your employees' resources can get you a long way, but when all is said and done, the reality is that excellent leadership is hard, tiring work, and it will take up a massive amount of time – including time that would otherwise be spent with your family.

However, it's your duty to see that the majority of your employees can balance family and work, which benefits the company and society at large.

Finding the right balance so that your company cultivates a healthy and ambitious working environment that promotes success is difficult, and I must admit that I myself still have plenty to learn in that regard.

I hope you can find this balance in your activities as a leader, and that you learn how to show tough love.

I do want to emphasise one thing, however, now that we're nearing the end of the book: successful leaders who can inspire employees to follow them through fire and water are always those who are comfortable with themselves, who know themselves and what they stand for.

The final chapter is therefore focused on what it means to be an authentic leader.

However, it's your duty to see that the majority of your employees can balance family and work, which benefits the company and society at large.

CHAPTER 8

Be Yourself

'TELL ME, have you gone completely nuts? You can't seriously be considering sending our plan back to Defence Command to see what they think of it!'

I was the chief of staff for the Danish battalion in Kosovo when, one day in March of 2005, I was confronted with this rather blunt question from the commander of the whole battalion.

'Well, yes ...' was my somewhat meek response. I had considered it. I definitely felt that our plan should be run by Defence Command, who would then distribute it to all the relevant parties so that the little details and nuances could be ironed out.

Before I arrived in Kosovo I had been at Defence Command for nearly three years, trained as a staff officer. Cases came in, were dealt with, submitted and presented. Then they came back again and were sent out for distribution and review, so that no stone would remain unturned. Finally, they landed back on my desk a third time, at which point I added comments like 'We cannot exclude the possibility that ...' or 'If the assumptions described here cannot be met, we must be prepared for ...'.

I was good at my job as a staff officer, really good, and I quickly learned to phrase the notes in a way that meant my reports moved relatively swiftly through the system, even at the highest level, where I was close to one of the generals. I had mastered the discipline, but now I was apparently nuts for behaving the same way in Kosovo!

The commander didn't mince words when it came to my 'staff officer approach', as he called it, explaining in no uncertain terms that it wasn't a good idea:

If I sent the case home for review, we would upset a lot of hard-working colleagues at Defence Command. They would get frustrated because they wouldn't know how to handle it, they'd circulate it among the staff and then the response we received would be so vaguely worded and full of hedging, 'do be aware'-type sentences that, all in all, it would be a major pain for both them and us. Didn't I see that?

'Well, yes ...' came my cautious reply.

His name was Colonel K.P. Pedersen, former commander of the Jaeger Corps, a Danish special operations force, and perhaps the officer from whom I learned the most when it came to being yourself as a leader. He became a crucial role model for me in the run-up to my next deployment as battle group commander in Afghanistan. Never before or since have I encountered a person so true to himself. He was the very definition of 'what you see is what you get', as they say when people aren't afraid to show who they are and what they stand for. We were well matched, and during the mission we developed a strong bond.

After thinking it over, I had to admit he was right. It didn't make sense to disturb other leaders with issues we were supposed to deal with ourselves. When you're chosen for a position of responsibility, it must be because the corporation's CEO, the director, the general, or whoever it might be, is confident that you can handle it.

Just a few days after this instructive conversation I suddenly heard K.P. yelling from his office, 'Kim, get in here now!'

Uh-oh, I thought, what have I done now? I didn't send anything to Defence Command, so that can't be it.

'Sit down and listen,' he said, slightly agitated. Then he picked up the phone and asked to speak to the Chief of Defence. I was starting to feel a little rattled – if I was about to be hauled over the coals while the Chief of Defence was on the line then I really wish he'd let me know beforehand.

After a brief pause he was put through to the Chief of Defence, Jesper Helsø. K.P. said, 'General, this is K.P. call-ing from Kosovo. I've got Kim Kristensen sitting in front of me so he can hear what we're saying.'

Helsø answered in his usual fashion – it sounded as if he were calmly puffing on his pipe: 'Fine, Klaus. What's this about?'

'I want this to be loud and clear. Kim is talented enough to take charge of the battalion if you no longer have confi-dence in me. That's why I'm calling. Just tell me straight if you've lost confidence in me. I'll pack my bags and hand command over to Kim.'

I had no idea what was going on, and evidently neither did Jesper Helsø. It emerged that K.P. had just received a letter from Defence Command in which something had been awkwardly answered in a manner that could be per-ceived as showing a lack of faith in his judgement, and he wasn't about to stand for that.

For me it was a revelation, I must admit. Ringing up the Chief of Defence and bluntly spelling out his point of view seemed utterly reckless. As I mentioned earlier, my previous position was as a staff officer, where there were many rungs above me. If I wanted to contact the Chief of Defence I had to go through the formal chain of command: first my head of division, then the head of department, then the head of the planning division, then the chief of the defence staff and finally the Chief of Defence himself.

K.P. put down the phone after Helsø had reassured him of his support, looked at me – I may have been a little pale at this point – and said, 'Nobody's going to bloody well shit all over me!'

No one in our unit was in any doubt as to where the boss stood, and nobody was in any doubt that he would fight their corner. Once you'd got to know him, and you quickly did, you were seldom surprised at his ideas, whims and broadsides. He was easy to read, which lent an enormous sense of calm to the organisation. Of course, he did also come up with a few crazy ideas, and when I confronted him with their repercussions he used to give a cheeky smile and say, 'Dammit, I didn't think you'd find out about that.'

As a soldier in the Jaeger Corps there's no question that he had got to know himself the hard way. The training in our special operations units is deliberately geared towards uncovering both strengths and weaknesses, and then eliminating the weaknesses. This process naturally makes people realise who they are, and what kind of human being they want to be. This training is for a select few individuals, and we others can simply try to learn from and be inspired by these elite soldiers – both personally and professionally.

When I first met K.P. I immediately asked about his directive for training and the mission in Kosovo. I was used to taking notes, writing letters and reports, so I took it as a given that he had written down a lot of his thoughts about our mission.

He looked at me with an incredulous expression. A directive? No, he hadn't really thought about that. But I must be reasonably competent, given that I had been assigned to 'look after him' over the coming months, so why didn't I just make a few suggestions?

Er, I hadn't seen that coming, but fair enough. It gave me a certain freedom, and I certainly had a few ideas about how to formulate a directive.

As we parted I suddenly heard him say, 'Wait, actually I do have a directive you should think about.'

I grabbed my pen and made ready to jot down a few pearls of wisdom. After all, something was better than nothing.

'You have to make me look good.'

'What the hell is he thinking?' I wondered during the hours after this somewhat arrogant pronouncement. But, over the following days and weeks, I reflected on what he had said, emerging with a rather more nuanced view of it. Arrogant K.P. was definitely not, and today I would say that his words were brilliant in their simplicity.

As chief of staff, making sure that the commander (and therefore the battalion) came across well was absolutely one of the most important parts of my job. I had to get rid of potential messes and present him with carefully considered, constructive solutions. He mustn't be troubled with unnecessary details, and should in fact be shielded from them so that he could concentrate on taking the strategically important decisions.

If I managed to keep all the crap away from him, he could interact with the unit and be there for the soldiers. He could be seen, which is a crucial factor in effective and

FOLLOW ME | CHAPTER 8

visible leadership. An organisation that doesn't sense the presence of its leader develops a distanced relationship with him. And who wants to follow a leader they don't know or feel anything for?

Nobody.

An organisation that doesn't sense the presence of its leader develops a distanced relationship with him. And who wants to follow a leader they don't know or feel anything for?

I could keep coming up with examples of K.P.'s leadership style as commander, but instead I'm just going to say that he was enormously significant for my personal development. He completely rid me of my staff-officer mentality at exactly the right moment, enabling me to prepare myself to lead in Afghanistan. There's a time for review and a time for decisions; in times of crisis and of war many decisions have to be taken – and quickly – so there isn't always time to distribute them for approval.

As I mentioned above, K.P.'s background as an elite soldier gave him a head start, but what about the rest of us? How do you get to the point where you can 'be yourself' in everything you do as a leader? Where everything is imbued with a sense of balance and of being comfortable in your own skin? Is it innate? Does it come with time? Can it be learned through training or education? It's complicated – of course it is – but I do have some observations about it that I would like to share.

From a purely professional perspective, the very best leaders I have seen operating first-hand have been stunningly competent within their area of expertise, whether that's technology, shipping, administration in local government or their job in a tank platoon. They have also mastered all the theoretical tools of leadership that might be of use them, but what makes them extraordinary is that they radiate a sense of calm, which is essential, and that they have what it takes to get people behind them.

When I look at the training and education many leaders undergo – at business schools, universities, military academies and schools of public administration, among other institutions – I can't help thinking about these three factors: professional competence, theoretical understanding of leadership and personal leadership. All three ingredients are essential to creating world-class leaders. But are they all at the same high level?

What I mean is that, in general, we have a system of education that adequately equips us in terms of professional skills. We can tick that box. When I look around the leadership landscape, I usually see plenty of professional competence.

I also believe that leaders usually have a good theoretical understanding of the tools of leadership and of what it takes to be effective, so we can more or less tick that box too.

But when it comes to developing the personal and human qualities that make a good leader, we don't go about it in anything like such a systematic and professional manner. Here, I think a warning light or a thumbs-down would be more apt than a tick. We don't emphasise enough that leaders should, on a personal level, radiate calm, self-confidence and self-awareness.

If you acknowledge the premise that truly superlative leaders should know themselves inside out, you must also ask the question: 'What can we do to support that? What can I myself do in terms of the leaders I'm responsible for?'

You have no idea how often I have been asked critical questions along the lines of: 'Are you saying we should all be in group therapy, then?', 'Isn't that a bit hippyish and woolly?' or 'Next you're going to tell us we all need to see a psychologist, aren't you?'

But the funny thing is that when we discuss the basic premises of extremely good leadership, taking a dull, dry, analytical approach, we somehow always end up saying that the leader has to know himself and has to be comfortable in his own skin. And once we've agreed on that, the important discussion begins in earnest. Because if we're right, what must be done in practical terms to follow up on this insight?

When we discuss the basic premises of extremely good leadership, taking a dull, dry, analytical approach, we somehow always end up saying that the leader has to know himself and has to be comfortable in his own skin.

I'm not saying that we all need a life coach or business psychologist by our side throughout our education and our working lives. No, if we're lucky enough to have role models to rely on – parents, teachers, coaches or bosses – then we can develop these personal qualities through a kind of apprenticeship. Leaders who have talent but aren't lucky enough to have the opportunity of an apprenticeship can nonetheless get a lot out of professional coaches, consultants and mentors.

And how significant are innate qualities? Are the most talented leaders born rather than made? Is it in their DNA?

I have known many people who made great strides towards a future career as a leader even in their childhood or youth. I have known many others who chose that path later on, and who developed into enormously good leaders. Much can therefore be learned.

Take a few minutes to think about whether you are wholly comfortable in your own skin as a leader. If you're not sure, it might be reassuring to know that I was in my mid forties before I could honestly say that I had reached that point. Should it really have taken me that long to feel that my actions were true to myself? Apparently!

How can it be that some leaders reach that point in their twenties or thirties, while for others it only happens as they approach fifty, or it never happens at all? Having spoken to many excellent leaders, I am convinced that it's down to parents, schooling and early life. It is there that the seeds of being true to yourself and having the self-confidence to develop are sown.

Many senior leaders have been accustomed to taking responsibility from their childhood. They were in the scouts or girl guides, coached sports teams or were president of the student council while holding down part-time jobs. I believe many talented leaders are shaped in their early youth. They store up the experiences that come with responsibility. Quietly and calmly, they acquire a certain set of values, coming to believe that decency, respect and involvement, but also a clear framework and direction, are the necessary elements of good leadership.

So if we want superlative leadership, we should pose the obvious question: do we pay enough attention to encouraging, developing and motivating young people towards leadership roles?

If you only start learning, when you're in your early twenties, about the crucial practical and personal qualities you need to be a good leader, you're already behind when it comes to the human factor.

So if we want superlative leadership, we should pose the obvious question: do we pay enough attention to encouraging, developing and motivating young people towards leadership roles?

You will be able to learn the professional and theoretical aspects very quickly, and you may get excellent marks in management, but if you don't have a store of experiences and knowledge to draw on then your practical leadership skills will suffer.

Of course, this isn't a reason to give up before you even start. These things can still be learned if you are aware of them or are made aware of them. You have a head start if you've been captain of the football team or a student rep at school, but in the long term this sort of 'muscle memory' from your youth isn't the be all and end all. The important thing is that you are aware of any gaps in your leadership skills and are willing to work on them.

What demands will be made on leaders in the future? I think it's only fair that I should try to offer a perspective on that.

Let us therefore return to one of the greatest military thinkers of the past, Carl von Clausewitz.

He pointed out that the complexity characteristic of war means that you cannot rely on systems and formulae. War is unpredictable by nature; we must understand and accept it as a social phenomenon.

In trying to describe the framework and conditions that need to be in place in order to truly excel as a leader, I have drawn inspiration from Clausewitz's teachings.

I am convinced that true excellence requires leaders who have the freedom to be themselves. Who aren't forced into a mechanical, technical mode of leadership or squeezed into a cookie-cutter leadership role. The more I have engaged with leadership, the clearer it has become that leaders who have limited room for manoeuvre can get acceptable results – but no more.

Perhaps the most dramatic thing for me has been to find that there is nothing new under the sun. There has been no elixir or magic spell discovered in our modern age to create the ideal, perfect leader.

The thinkers of the past – both military and non-military – have already given us the recipe for leadership that achieves outstanding results. Ultimately, philosophers, the Bible and modern leadership gurus are saying the same thing – and fundamentally, it comes down to decency and self-knowledge.

The philosopher Søren Kierkegaard was right to note that one must be a human being first and a leader second.

As I see it, one of the biggest challenges for future leaders will therefore be getting to know themselves and doing all they can to become whole, well-rounded people.

When all is said and done, leadership is a social activity. It's about people getting other people to perform at a high level. Succeeding at that does not involve much hocus pocus in terms of practical leadership; it has always been hard work, requiring a framework to develop, motivate and inspire employees to do their best. Your personality will therefore have an enormous influence on the results your employees achieve.

As I see it, one of the biggest challenges for future leaders will therefore be getting to know themselves and doing all they can to become whole, well-rounded people.

Another challenge we will all face in the future is that everything will happen at breakneck speed. This means we must be flexible, ready to readjust at a moment's notice, with a positive attitude to risk-taking and the ability to 'love chaos'.

The companies, institutions, organisations and countries that don't recognise this – remaining weighed down by their heavy regulatory and control mechanisms – will gradually grind to a halt and end up being left behind, with unmotivated employees. They are the future losers.

Other future losers will include bosses and managers who try to persuade their employees that rationalisation and improvements in efficiency that save millions, or even billions, are a gift for the company.

A gift?

This is especially worrying when those same bosses and managers seem to think that, despite the cutbacks that have been implemented, they can and will achieve the same results.

Who are they trying to convince?

If these leaders think they're seeing credible and confidence-building leadership in the mirror, then it's time to clean the glass. They're not convincing their employees, and if they don't present the consequences of the cutbacks in a straightforward and forthcoming manner to their own superiors then they will eventually be found out.

I have, incidentally, never understood how people can dare claim that they will be able to achieve the same results with far fewer resources. If this were really the case, they should have pointed it out much earlier.

Cutbacks that save millions or billions have consequences. Everybody understands that. Just be honest about it, and then let's see what we have left in the toolbox to accomplish what we're supposed to. It's only fair.

The fundamental principles of warfare – as formulated by Clausewitz – always hold true. They emphasise the significance of focusing on your goal, of being on the offensive, of surprise and effectiveness and of being economical with your resources. If you bear these fundamental principles in mind, while making sure that individual leaders have the necessary balance between freedom and responsibility, you can secure outstanding results for the future.

We should invest in leadership that allows us to act sensibly in response to ongoing challenges. Once the right

framework and intentions are in place, we will need leaders who dare to be role models.

When I left Defence Command in 2004 to prepare for the
mission in Kosovo, I was given a parting bit of advice by
General Per Ludvigsen:
'Take decisions!'
It was the only thing he really said to me. Strange, I
thought. And a bit thin.
But the general knew exactly what he was talking about.
For many years I had been handling cases, and had turned
into a real 'process officer'. Now he wanted to remind me
that my new role would require more decisiveness and a
little extra vigour.
Chew these two words over: 'Take decisions!'
They have been with me ever since, in all their simplicity. They have challenged me constantly, and now I'm
passing them on to you.
As a leader, you must be willing to take decisions when
needed, even when chaos reigns.
If those decisions are to be effective and successful,
your professional competence must be top-notch, and you
must ensure the right framework is in place for you and
your employees.
You must be prepared to lead from the front, picking up
the heaviest rucksack.
You must behave ethically and morally, so that you can
live with yourself for the rest of your life, no matter what
happens.

You must know yourself, so that you can be sincere in showing consideration for your employees.

The choice is yours. What kind of leader do you want to be?

It takes great courage to be an authentic and strong leader – a leader who employees will be queuing up to follow.

Are you courageous?

Testimonials

'*Follow Me* is about leadership – in life and death situations! A gripping account of the process of developing personal leadership, where failure means the loss of human life! My own job mainly deals with life – with developing and selling products that save lives – but there's also the risk that if we don't get it right we might cost people their lives! I wish I had had these general recipes for leadership when I first started out, and I can confirm that the principles are generally applicable, although I myself mostly learned through trial and error! My biggest "aha" moment came when I reached the description of how important intuition is as a basis for taking decisions under extreme pressure. Intuition is the "collected memory of all our experiences", which we can draw on without thinking about it when time is short – and it's never let me down yet ...'

LARS REBIEN SØRENSEN
CEO Novo Nordisk, 2000–2017, voted World's Best CEO 2015 & 2016 (Harvard Business Review)

'A strong book about the essential issues surrounding leadership. And who better to write such a book than an officer who has had to carry out the ultimate responsibility of setting goals and guidelines for people in wartime, creating confidence and maintaining focus – without getting too involved in the details. Whether you are a leader in uniform during wartime or make your income in the world of industry, the roles, challenges and demands are the same. Definitely worth a read for anyone who is or wants to become a leader.'

JESPER HELSØ
General, Chief of Defence, Denmark, 2002–2008

It is my great pleasure to give Kim Kristensen's book Follow Me my highest recommendation. Leadership is about serving the community. It is about taking responsibility for decisions made on behalf of that community. Kristensen's book is a powerful, experience-based testament to what it means to show authority as a leader. It is also an incredibly compelling narrative. Kim is an outstanding communicator – both on paper and in person. I hope this book will benefit many readers across the world. It deserves to.'

LENE TANGGAARD PEDERSEN

Ph.D., Professor and Director of The Centre for Qualitative Studies, Department of Communication & Psychology, Aalborg University

'The book uses examples to demonstrate what a frontline leader's role is: to take decisions and build credibility by leading from the front and being a good example. In doing so it also illustrates senior leaders' most important responsibilities, which are to assemble the right team of well-prepared leaders and trust them to make the right decisions, even if the analytical basis is lacking. The value of trust and credibility right the way up an organisation is clearly illustrated throughout the whole book.'

NILS SMEDEGAARD ANDERSEN

CEO A.P. Moeller-Maersk, 2007–2016

'A leader must be able to map out and explain the direction. "What is the purpose of what we're doing?" And "what is the role of the individual in a larger context?" This book offers good examples of how an organisation's resources can be realised and made the most of when its leader sets a course and creates breathing space for the levels below.'

PETER BARTRAM

General, Chief of Defence, Denmark, 2012–2017

'Engaged employees are the shortest way to satisfied customers, and as such to successful business. At ISS we find great inspiration in Mr Kristensen's leadership perspectives based on his experience from extreme situations. Follow me: Leading from the Front can easily be related to a commercial setting and is a fantastic collection of examples of the value of having leaders, who lead by example and are empowered to take action together with their dedicated and engaged employees in the front line directly facing the customers. In short, the book describes a set of universal leadership principles relevant to leaders and managers across sectors and functions.'

JEFF GRAVENHORST
Group CEO, ISS A/S

'*Follow Me* is one of the only leadership books I have read where I really feel that it's an authentic and relevant leader who's talking. Kim Kristensen knows himself and his values so well that he is able to lead even the toughest missions. He leads from the front, maps out a strategy and sets goals, and most important of all – his employees follow him. The book depicts an unusually strong and charismatic leader who posses-ses some of the most important qualities I believe a good leader should possess: the ability to lead from the front, especially when doing so is difficult, the ability to be considerate towards employees and the ability to give employees something and someone to stand up for. A fantastic role model for his employees and an ambassador for good leadership. Kim Kristensen emphasises that there is one principle of leadership that overshadows all the others, and that is the principle of leading by exam-ple. This in itself should be an argument for reading the book, which is a goldmine of practical advice. An inspiring book on personal leadership, which I can warmly recommend to leaders at all levels.'

VIBEKE SKYTTE
Director, The Danish Association of Managers and Executives

Kim Kristensen manages to revitalise the classic leader without becoming authoritarian or clichéd. He emphasises the significance of standing out as a clear figurehead with the power to act and make decisions, and not "just" being a team player. He advocates for solidarity in the sense that a leader must invest in confidence and in building strong relationships in order to obtain the social capital that is a prerequisite for being visible and being able to act as a clear figurehead. It is a lesson all leaders should learn, because without it you will end up casting around for something else to focus your energies on as a leader.'

JAN MOLIN

Professor and Dean of Copenhagen Business School, Denmark

'A very personal book, which draws the reader into a world that for most people lies far outside their everyday comfort zone. An exciting and compelling story from a perspective where familiar leadership strategies are taken to a level where leaders are constantly being faced with unfamiliar factors. The world today is a complex place, where global events have a big impact on national issues. This means that leaders today must be able to interpret and act in accordance with these manifold issues – closely corresponding to Kim Kristensen's experience as a leader.'

KIM STAACK NIELSEN

MBA and Diploma in Business Administration, Chairman of DANISH HR

'This is a trustworthy book, and it is about trust. Trust in employees and trust in the importance of leadership. The message is clear: as a leader and manager you cannot escape the imperative of walking the talk – the motivation of your employees is directly linked with your trust in them and with your own legitimacy. For changes to become meaningful you need to put yourself at stake.'

KURT KLAUDI KLAUSEN

Professor, Director of MPM, Department of Political Science and Public Management, University of Southern Denmark

'I think this is a good choice for the 2015 Leadership Book of the Year. It's a well-written, accessible and easy-to-read book that can be read both as an exciting insight into the concrete experiences of a specific leader and as a great source of inspiration for your own reflections on leadership. What I think is especially good about this book is that it includes many concrete examples, and although they are drawn from wartime experiences (or similar), Kim Kristensen succeeds in "translating" them into principles applicable to the world of business. Yet he doesn't take it too far – the thing that's so inspiring about the book is that it provides examples while making readers think for themselves about how they can be applied to their own leadership situation.

It's difficult to choose one single thing that inspired me or that I can use. I think the whole book is inspirational, and overall I very much agree with the points Kim makes. But I could perhaps emphasise the point about leading from the front and being a role model – and about giving employees an understanding of not just a goal, but a purpose. That, I think, is absolutely fundamental to leadership. I also found the section on training like you fight a source of inspiration. I believe we can learn a lot from the very systematic focus on training and education that Kim describes.'

HENRIETTE FENGER ELLEKROG

Senior Executive Vice President, Head of Group HR, Danske Bank

According to Kim Kristensen, one principle of leadership overshadows all the others: the principle of leading by example. And I could not agree with him more. It's easy to say, "Follow me" when things are trundling along nicely, but what engenders confidence and credibility is saying and – above all – doing it when things look bleak. Your employees should feel that they have something and someone to stand up for – it's that simple.'
TORBEN BALLEGAARD SØRENSEN
Former CEO of B&O. Author of The Value Adding Board and board member with Vestas A/S and Egmont International A/S

Follow Me is about being an authentic leader – not just an authority figure. It's a book about getting people to follow you on the basis of trust and credibility, and the ability to lead during tough times. One of the most inspirational books about leadership I have read – worth following!'
JIM HAGEMANN SNABE
Chairman of the Board, A.P. Moeller-Maersk and former Group CEO of SAP. Board member of the World Economic Forum, Siemens, Allianz and Bang & Olufsen. Snabe is adjunct professor at Copenhagen Business School, CBS, Denmark

'Highly recommendable ... Highlights that strategic thinking and management by the good example creates extraordinary results through dedicated employees. Proves that good leadership is generic.'
PETER HØJLAND
Former CEO of SAS Denmark and Superfos A/S. Chairman of Siemens Denmark A/S and 'Wonderful Copenhagen'

'Why should somebody choose to follow me?' This is a question all leaders should put to themselves. You're made a boss from above, but chosen as a leader from below. Leadership makes a difference, and leaders with an active group of followers have the right foundation to get the results they want. Kim Kristensen has been a natural leader for most of his life, often in the most incredibly demanding situations. Offering practical examples drawn from some of the world's most volatile places, Kim Kristensen illustrates the significance of having faith in your employees and of clear communication in an open, honest, compelling and gripping manner. This insight – and many, many other lessons in the book – will prove inspirational for anybody who wants others to follow them.'

CHRISTIAN KURT NIELSEN

CEO / Chairman of the Board of Mercuri Urval